"I've frequently referred to Tony Hall—jokingly—as my favorite Democrat. He has had the courage all these years to stand virtually alone in his party in defense of life. He has been one of the most principled and effective congressman, focusing particularly on issues of world hunger and human rights. As I've come to know Tony personally my respect for him has grown. He is the real thing—a political figure who puts his Christian faith to work. If you want to put your faith to work, this book will inspire and move you. Tony Hall makes a clear and powerful witness of the transforming power of Christ in a man's life."

— Charles W. Colson
Founder and Chairman,
Prison Fellowship

"A wonderful book by a wonderful man! It takes us with him as he visits the poor of the world, and tells what we must do to respond to their needs if we are to be faithful Christians."

— Tony Campolo
Professor of Psychology,
Eastern University
Author of *Speaking My Mind*

"Whether serving in Congress or as Ambassador to the U.N. food and agriculture agencies, Tony Hall has been a great friend and advocate for humanitarian organizations dedicated to fighting poverty and hunger around the world. This memoir is a testament to his commitment to action in alleviating poverty, as well as a primer on how all Americans can get involved. He challenges each of us to follow the simple wisdom of Mother Teresa: To do the thing that's in front of you."

— Ken Hackett
President,
Catholic Relief Services

"This is the only book I've recommended in common with Cal Thomas and Chuck Colson, except for the G. Gordon Liddy workout book. Tony Hall is a hero to the widest spectrum of Americans and citizens of the world, because of who he is and what he's done for the poor. I urge everyone to read this fascinating and inspiring book."

— AL FRANKEN
Comedian, talk show host,
Author of *The Truth (with jokes)* and
other best-selling books

"*Changing the Face of Hunger* will hopefully do just that. Tony Hall has been an inspiration for years to me and others committed to doing what they can to bring justice to the hungry. His stories and experiences prove that one person can make a difference. His witness and leadership in Congress were a true example for others of using a position of power to help the powerless. Hopefully this great book will contribute to building the public will necessary to end hunger and poverty in our country and around the world."

— DAVID BECKMANN
President, Bread for the World;
Alliance to End Hunger

"Ending Hunger requires us to put aside our differences and work together. Tony is a great example of someone who has done this successfully."

— JEFF BRIDGES
Actor

"Hunger knows no language, no race, no class, no gender. It is the deprivation of the body and starvation of the soul. Tony Hall discovered that when one of us is hungry, we all are in need. When we deny people food, we are robbing them of the most basic of human rights. This is the story of one man, one human being who urges the whole human family to take a stand, to reach out to our brothers and sisters who are suffering all around us and begin the rise of a compassionate world community"

— JOHN LEWIS
U.S. Representative (D-Georgia),
Civil Rights Leader

CHANGING
THE FACE
OF HUNGER

CHANGING
THE FACE
OF HUNGER

TONY HALL

with **Tom Price**

W PUBLISHING GROUP
A Division of Thomas Nelson Publishers
Since 1798
www.wpublishinggroup.com

Published by W Publishing Group, a Division of Thomas Nelson, Inc., P.O. Box 141000, Nashville, Tennessee 37214.

W Publishing Group books may be purchased in bulk for educational, business, fund-raising, or sales promotional use. For information, please e-mail SpecialMarkets@ThomasNelson.com.

All Scripture quotations are taken from the New Revised Standard Version Bible, © 1989 by the Division of Christian Education of the National Council of the Churches of Christ in the USA. Used by permission. All rights reserved.

Page Design: Walter Petrie

Library of Congress Cataloging-in-Publication Data

Hall, Tony, 1951–
    The changing face of hunger / by Tony Hall.
        p. cm.
    ISBN 0-8499-0050-6
    1. Hunger—Religious aspects—Christianity. 2. Food supply—Religious aspects—Christianity. 3. Church and social problems. I. Title.
    BR115.H86H35 2006
    261.8'325—dc22   2005031465

Printed in the United States of America

06 07 08 09 10 QW 9 8 7 6 5 4 3 2 1

DEDICATION

Mostly, I dedicate this book to a wonderful "gift of God," the meaning of the name Matthew, our son, who God chose to go before us. He is a constant source of inspiration, and his bravery in his losing battle with cancer showed us how to live and how to die.

Also, I would like to dedicate this book to my wife Janet, who has walked through the valleys and mountains with me, and to our daughter, Jyl, who always inspires me and is a source of refreshment and renewal.

I heard the voice of the Lord saying,
"Whom shall I send, and who will go for us?"
And I said, "Here am I; send me!"

—ISAIAH 6:8

CONTENTS

Acknowledgments   xv

1. Ethiopia   1
Opening My Eyes, Filling My Heart

2. Brothers beyond Politics   15
Succeeding by Finding Common Ground

3. Walking with Mother Teresa   31
Doing What's in Front of Her

4. All in the Family   43
Doing What's in Front of Us

5. Romania   57
Faith Deposes Might

6. The Fast   71
Follow God, Lead by Example, and the People Will Respond

7. Bringing It All Back Home   91
Doing What's in Front of Dayton

8. The United States   103
*Finding and Fighting Hunger and Poverty Around the Corner
and Over the Hill*

9. Ripping Out the Roots of Terror   119
Our Good Works Will Make Us Safer

10. Everyone Is Called to Serve the Poor   135
Learning One Universal Truth

11. The Democratic Party   147
Finding Common Ground within Our Political Family

12. Where We Are Today   163
Noteworthy Progress but Still a Long Way to Go

13. New Orleans   181
America Discovers Its Invisible Poor

Appendix: How to Help   189

Notes   197

ACKNOWLEDGMENTS

O n the pages of my life, there have been many people who were always there for me and who helped make me look good.

I want first to thank my wife Janet and daughter Jyl for their constant love and encouragement; Dad, my two brothers Mike and Sam, and especially my mom, who always says "I love you." I also want to thank Janet's family; you couldn't ask for better in-laws..

Congressman Frank Wolf plays an important role in the pages of this book. For more than 20 years he and I fought the good fight together in Congress and had a darn good time at it. Thank you, Frank and Carolyn.

My buddies, Nick and Jody Sabatino, let me be me and provided a place over the years for me to do just that.

John Nakamura has been my prayer partner these past few years and has traveled the world with me. Thanks, John and Janice. And thanks to Marvin Marcus, who introduced me to my wife

To my staff in Congress and at the U.S. Mission to the U.N. Food and Agricultural Agencies in Rome: I want to thank each one of you for your loyalty and, for some of you, a great length of service. To single out just a few: Rick Carne, who started with me; Michael Gessel, a great press secretary; Ernie Loevinsohn who taught me most of what I know about hunger; Bonnie Ruestow, who served me so many years; Marty Rendon, Max Finberg, Deborah DeYoung, David Goldberg, George Lowrey, David Austin, Tom Studevant, Jim Vangrov, Bobby Turner, Gary Froelich, Bob Zachritz, Madeline Iseli, Ruth Snyder, Donna Riddlebarger, and Carol Prewitt. I also want to acknowledge the wonderful people who have carried on the vision of the Congressional Hunger Center, Ed Cooney and Margaret Zeigler.

Farley Chase, our agent, worked tirelessly to help us transform our ideas into a clear plan for writing this book. His colleague, Scott Waxman, contributed important advice. We are grateful that our publisher, David Moberg, saw the value in what we wanted to write. We thank the *Dayton Daily News*, for giving us access to its library, and the Kettering Foundation, for supporting Tom's research into the Community Council for the Homeless.

I especially want to thank the many people who have mentored me over the years and taught me the importance of trying to live the words of Jesus of Nazareth, including Jerry Regier, Roy Cook, Doug Coe, Margie and Chuck Wright, Barbara Priddy, Sam Hines, John Staggers, Tom Skinner, Jim Hutchins, Sam Owen, and Fred Heyn.

There have been so many other people along life's way who contributed a great deal to my life. Even though there is not space to mention all of you, I want you to know that I remember and I am grateful to you.

Chapter 1

ETHIOPIA

Opening My Eyes,
Filling My Heart

Viewed from the twin-engine prop plane making its way north from the capital of Addis Ababa to the village of Alamata in the rebel-controlled countryside, Ethiopia showed off a rugged, oddly beautiful landscape.

As Addis disappeared behind us, plains and plateaus gave way to ridges and peaks that thrust their sharp edges into the cloudless blue sky. Rifts in the mountains suggested miniature versions of America's Grand Canyon. The bright sun and clear sky heightened the stark beauty of the scene.

Here and there a patch of green stood out. But the overriding color scheme was made up of browns and grays. Dirt and dust dominated the land. The riverbeds were dry. Crops would not grow. Forests had been sacrificed for firewood. Tree roots had been dug up for food.

Ethiopia had suffered grievously from drought in the early 1970s. In the early 1980s, famine returned. Now, in November 1984, as I made my first trip to the country, I was told that even cacti could not survive in the dry earth.

I had heard reports that two hundred thousand Ethiopians had died already, nearly a million likely would die by the end of the year, and millions more were at risk. International relief groups were issuing alarming calls for help. Television news organizations were beaming disturbing pictures of hunger into homes in the United States and other Western countries. But none of this prepared me for what I was about to experience. I have often told people that as a public official, in order to understand a situation, I have to see it, walk around in it, walk in the shoes of the people who are there. To deal successfully with an issue, I have to develop a passion for it. Passion is what enables someone to become an effective advocate, to touch other people's hearts, to move other public officials, to get the public mobilized to want to do something. That is why I felt I needed to go to Ethiopia in 1984 and why I have gone to many other such places in the years since.

The plane on which I was traveling was ferrying supplies to a camp run by the World Vision Christian relief organization. Ernie Loevinsohn and I had hitched a ride from Addis, as had two members of Mother Teresa's Missionaries of Charity, who had a mission at World Vision's compound. We landed on Alamata's dirt airstrip, which, we were told, had to be swept for land mines each morning because of the civil war that was exacerbating Ethiopia's tragedy.

The relief compound was surrounded by barbed-wire fence, which seemed in stark contrast to the World Vision workers' dedication to serving the poor and the missionaries' commitment to living among the neediest. The barrier was necessitated, however, by the fact that relief workers were able to help only a fraction of the overwhelming number of desperate Ethiopians standing outside the fence and needing assistance.

Thousands of severely malnourished Ethiopians had made their way to Alamata and surrounded the compound, hoping for food and medical treatment. In addition to malnutrition, many also suffered from dehydration, dysentery, malaria, cholera, and tuberculosis. We were told that dozens had died of starvation or related illnesses outside the compound overnight. Inside, three children had died just before we arrived that morning. A doctor—a Brit or an Australian, I judged by his accent—was about to make his morning rounds. He invited me to join him.

As we walked through the crowd outside the compound, hundreds of hungry people grabbed at our hands and tugged at our pant legs, begging for help. Many of the adults held up their children, trying to thrust them into our arms. They understood what the doctor was doing. Because supplies were severely limited, he explained to me, he could provide treatment for starvation to only a half dozen children each day.

"I have to pick six or seven kids that we can save," he said. The ones who seemed most likely to recover if treated would be nurtured through the several stages of recovery from starvation, receiving the food and medicine they needed. Most of the rest of the starving would die within days.

As I watched the doctor choose his next handful of patients and pass over the many, I thought of my own children, Jyl and Matt, who were eight and four at the time, the same ages as many of the starving youngsters who surrounded me. I fished my sunglasses out of my shirt pocket and put them on, as I would many times over the next few days—not to protect my eyes from the tropical sun, but to hide my tears. I would soon discover that things were even worse elsewhere.

World Vision had found a Jeep and a driver to take Ernie and me to our next destination, Korem, a village that was a one- to two-hour drive north of Alamata. NBC correspondent Peter Dent joined us.

Our Jeep was the only motor vehicle on the dirt road that wound its way up the hills to the plateau on which Korem sits. We passed some walkers and an occasional well-off person on a donkey, but mostly we were alone. The view on the ground confirmed my impressions from the air. The landscape was rugged, rocky, and brown. Everything was dry. Nothing grew.

Ethiopia had been in a state of perpetual civil war for years. The overthrow of Emperor Haile Selassie in 1974 had led to the establishment of an oppressive Communist dictatorship that was opposed by regional armies, especially in the north where we were traveling. The warfare compounded the effects of the famine as the government diverted relief supplies to its troops, and the fighting disrupted attempts by relief organizations to deliver supplies to the starving. These facts were at the forefront of our minds when we crested a hill and heard loud automatic-weapons fire nearby.

Our driver jammed on the brakes, turned off the ignition, and bolted from the Jeep. Nearby pedestrians dived into the roadside ditches, so Peter, Ernie, and I did the same. After lying in the dust for a few moments, I stuck my head up to look for our driver. People nearby screamed at me. Although I didn't understand their language, I knew immediately that they were telling me to keep my head down.

The gunfire continued sporadically for a while. We had no reason to believe it was aimed at us, but it was unnerving nevertheless. Lying there in the dust, we were filthy and we were scared. Finally, after about ten minutes of silence, we decided to move.

We ran for the Jeep. With our driver nowhere in sight, I jumped behind the steering wheel and took off, speeding as fast as I could, leaving a cloud of sand and dust and rocks behind us. Nobody told me to slow down. When we approached Korem, however, our apparent brush with Ethiopia's civil war lost all sense of significance. In a day of repeated shocks, this was beyond anything imaginable.

I had seen poverty as a Peace Corps volunteer in Thailand. As a member of Congress, I had made hunger one of my top concerns. I had helped to establish the House Select Committee on Hunger and had become chairman of the committee's International Task Force. I had sought to understand the extent of poverty and hunger in my congressional district in Dayton, Ohio. And this was not my first congressional fact-finding trip to the third world. But I had never seen anything like this. And neither had Ernie, the Staff Director of the hunger committee, who had worked for years in international relief organizations.

Tens of thousands of starving people had walked—some up to 150 miles—to get to this high, bleak plateau, having heard that food, water, clothing, and blankets would be distributed here. But their demand for help had so quickly exceeded the available relief supplies that there was essentially nothing for most of them. So they just waited, hoping for assistance that would not arrive until days after our visit. Because this was a large, flat expanse of land, it was possible to take in the entire scene at once, and it was overwhelming.

The sky was pure blue, the sun piercing. The temperature was 75 or 80 degrees—a perfect California afternoon. Except that here all the land was brown and dusty. And forty thousand to fifty thousand people were encamped here—some in makeshift tents, some in grass huts, some in wooden sheds that relief organizations had erected for the most severely ill, but most in the open. All were malnourished, some closer to death than others. They wore dusty, rough robes. Some appeared nearly naked, their clothing was so worn. Flies lit on their bodies, and they were too feeble to brush them away. They were docile, weak to the point of exhaustion because they had no food and because the cold nights further drained their nearly nonexistent energy. While Ethiopia is a tropical country, nighttime temperatures can drop to near freezing on this high plateau.

Perhaps what struck me most from the distance was the sound. Children cried. Women wailed. The sick coughed. But mostly the air was filled with an eerie, low moan. Thousands of people had simply come to the end. They just lay there, and they suffered, and they moaned, and they died.

We were told that fifty-six people had died the day before we arrived, and sixty-one the day before that. A week earlier, the death toll averaged more than one hundred people a day. The bodies would be carried to the edge of the encampment and laid out. I had never seen anyone die before. That day at Korem, I witnessed twenty-five children's deaths in the few hours we were there.

As I walked among the people, I was drawn to the children. Teenagers, weighing fifty pounds or less, were so wrinkled they could be mistaken for the elderly. I saw an eight-year-old child who weighed twenty-three pounds. These children had the distended bellies that are the telltale sign of extreme hunger. Every bone could be counted. When they died, they just stopped breathing. If a child was with his or her mother, you'd then see the mother react, sometimes with nothing but resignation, sometimes with deep grief. Some mothers hugged their dead children tightly; some lay down beside their children and sobbed. As I walked, I saw this happen again and again. Perhaps worst of all, I saw children die alone, saw adults die alone.

Our runaway driver sheepishly showed up at Korem, head down, appearing embarrassed that he had deserted us on the road. He took us back to Alamata, where Ernie and I climbed into the same World Vision plane to fly back to Addis. I sat by myself at a window, staring at the countryside below and struggling to comprehend the horror I had seen.

That night Ernie and I were invited to dinner at the home of the U.S. chargé d'affaires. Because the U.S. government disapproved of Ethiopia's Communist government, we did not have an ambassador in Addis at the time.

The chargé was away, so Ernie and I had the elegant mansion to ourselves. We had showered, scrubbed the day's dirt and dust from our bodies, and put on clean clothes. Now we were being led into a large dining room with a long banquet table that was set with beautiful silver and china and decorated with fresh-cut flowers.

Ethiopian waiters in white jackets and white gloves served us a lavish meal. I can't recall the exact menu, but the meal included salad, meat, potatoes, vegetables, bread, butter, wine, and a selection of desserts. I know we could have had seconds if we'd asked.

Ernie and I sat there, looking at each other, looking at all this food, and thinking about what we had seen just a few hours earlier. This meal, prepared for the two of us, would have fed one hundred or more of the hungry at Alamata or Korem.

Neither of us could eat. We didn't feel like talking. So we pushed back from the table and went to our rooms for the rest of the night.

I called Janet, my wife, and tried to explain what I had seen that day. But it was too hard. I couldn't talk. I tried to read, which is what I normally do at the end of the day, but I couldn't do that either. So I just sat on my bed and thought.

The next day I encountered stark evidence of the way that Alamata and Korem had changed my perspective on the world. We flew south this time, to visit a relief center serving the seminomadic Bume people near Ethiopia's border with Sudan.

Once again we flew over a brown, arid land. When we were on the ground, we again were told how there had been little rain, the river had dried up, the harvest had failed, and the Bume's primary food source at this time was the roots of trees. We saw naked children with swollen bellies. One mother told us how each family would give one or two children the responsibility of keeping the family supplied with water. They would have to walk long distances with buckets to a source of drinkable water. Sometimes a child would walk most of the day to obtain the water and take it back home.

But there was little sickness. The children had not yet descended into a severe state of malnutrition. The nakedness was normal: the Bume, children and adults, wore little or no clothing all the time. World Vision had built a warehouse, and people said food would be on the way.

I thought to myself, *This isn't as bad as I expected it would be.*

But, of course, it would be very bad if the food didn't arrive soon. And I worried about the people we couldn't visit because they lived in the extreme backcountry, beyond airstrips and roads and international relief organizations.

It was not until we were on the airplane during the long flight home that I could begin to sort out and make sense of what we had seen.

This was, of course, a natural disaster. Drought had caused a famine that was causing millions of people to go hungry. And this was not an unprecedented occurrence. The region is susceptible to frequent droughts. Earthquakes, volcanic eruptions, and locust swarms are also recurring parts of the environment. When the current drought began to take its toll in the early 1980s, the nation was still suffering the effects of a great drought-caused famine from the early 1970s. The sequence of drought, famine, hunger, and starvation had been repeated in Ethiopia for centuries.

But there was more to it than that. Desperation and ignorance led to poor farming practices that exacerbated water shortages and caused deforestation, soil erosion, and desertification. The repressive Communist government did not want the world to learn of its troubles and had tried to hide the extent of the disaster, which was compounded by the regime's ideological economic policies. The civil war was killing tens of thousands of people outright, disrupting aid efforts, and creating hundreds of thousands of refugees. As part of its military campaign against the rebels, the government was blocking relief shipments to rebel-controlled areas as well as stealing food in order to feed its army. The wealthy world was taking too long to understand the need and too long to respond.

In addition to making visits to the Ethiopian backcountry, Ernie and I were able to meet with relief workers in Addis.

One man, named Solomon, described and illustrated the human-caused aspects of the disaster. He had spent a year and a half in jail because he refused to pledge allegiance to the Marxist doctrine of the government. He also was persecuted, he said, because of his Christian faith, and some three hundred Christian leaders were still in jail. He believed that Ethiopia was suffering because the government had turned its back on God, but that the suffering would make the people strong.

Others confirmed some of the gruesome stories we had heard about Ethiopian dictator Mengistu Haile Mariam. It's true, they said, that he kept lions in the basement of his palace—visitors could hear them roar. He used them to frighten prisoners during interrogations and to frighten the Ethiopian people into staying in line.

One of the most astounding things we learned from our conversations in Addis was that the residents of Ethiopia's capital did not know the extent to which malnutrition, hunger, and death existed in their country. Their ability to travel was restricted, and their news media were controlled by the government, so they were kept in the dark.

Another thing we learned was that Ethiopia's needs were broad. While food was required immediately, we were told, it had to be the right food. And food alone would not solve this nation's enormous problems.

Two kinds of nutrition aid were needed. Now, and for a long time even after the famine finally passed, many Ethiopians would lack basic rations, such as grain, to feed their families. The malnourished and starving urgently needed special feeding regimens and medical treatment to nurture them back to health. There was great demand for medicines to treat the sick, as well as vaccinations and inoculations to protect all Ethiopians from diseases that had been conquered in the developed world. Many also needed blankets and tents. And the relief organizations required trucks to carry the supplies to the far-flung suffering communities. To prevent the endless recurrence of drought, famine, and death, relief efforts would have to include the drilling of water wells, the construction of irrigation projects, and the education of primitive farmers in effective and sustainable agricultural practices.

I spent my time on the flight home just as I had on that flight from Alamata to Addis Ababa within Ethiopia—in a window seat, staring outside. The protective shock was wearing off, and I was having difficulty coping with what I had seen over the last several days. It wasn't just the human suffering that I found so disturbing, but also the human cruelty that had helped to cause the suffering and was delaying relief. It's something I've never been able to completely come to grips with—how humans can treat one another with such inhumanity. Here we were, in the closing years of the supposedly civilized, supposedly modern twentieth century, and we were in the process of killing more people in that one modern, civilized century than in the entire previous history of humankind.

In retrospect, I can see that many of the problems I would deal with over the coming two decades were thrown at me during that one trip to Ethiopia: drought, famine, hunger, starvation, illness, lack of shelter, lack of clothing, political oppression, religious persecution, war, hatred. I encountered the seeds of solutions as well: the dedicated workers in private aid agencies, religious relief organizations, and government assistance programs; the advocates for human rights and humanitarian assistance; and the enormous power of the news media to call the world's attention to a problem and inspire action to solve it. If it hadn't been for the BBC's pioneering reporting in Ethiopia, the response from the developed world would have come even later. If other media hadn't followed with their reporting, the food, medical, and developmental assistance would not have been as robust or as effective.

It was to those signs of hope that my thoughts turned as the large commercial airliner carried me toward home.

I recalled the World Vision workers and Missionaries of Charity at Alamata. Every day, they were able to save maybe a half dozen children out of thousands of people who were gathered around them and pleading for help. It would be easy to look at that effort and wonder, *What's the point? That's such an insignificant number when so many are suffering.* But if the relief workers weren't there at all, no one would have been saved. And if they were saving six a day, that's more than forty a week. And as the weeks rolled on, you'd be talking about hundreds.

While I was at Alamata, one of the sisters asked me if I'd like to see their generator room. I wondered why, in this scene of suffering and death, she'd want to show me a generator. I followed her into a hut with a twig roof and a dirt floor and discovered that the "generator room" was their chapel. It was here they came to pray, renewing themselves for their difficult tasks every day. They called it their generator room because it was where they restored their power to go on with their work.

That led me to think about a discussion I'd had shortly before I began my trip to Ethiopia.

I had, for a few years, been meeting weekly in Washington with a small group of men to pray and discuss the Scriptures. One day, one of the men in the group said to me, "Tony, don't you think it's time you brought God into your workplace?"

It was a question that troubled me a great deal. I was becoming a strong believer, and my faith was becoming the central driving force in my life, including being the prime motivator of my involvement in humanitarian issues such as hunger. But this faith was relatively new to me, and I was highly uneasy about flaunting it in public.

My workplace was Congress and the broader field of politics and public affairs. Although I made no secret of the growing importance of faith in my life—including my public life—I told reporters who covered me that I did not want to wear it on my sleeve and I had no intention of shoving it down other people's throats. I had seen too many public people profess their faith and then not live up to their words. I had seen people talk about God to advance their own purposes, then cause faith to be diminished in others' eyes when their hypocrisy was exposed.

I wanted to do what my friend suggested it was time for me to do. But I didn't know how. On this flight out of Ethiopia, I found the answer.

I thought about how, in a political career, you can flit from campaign to campaign, from issue to issue, and really accomplish nothing. I thought about how we do so many things in our lives—so many things in Congress—that amount to nothing, how a good portion of our time is wasted. Because I often talked about the importance of passion, I asked myself what I was passionate about and realized that many of those passions didn't amount to much.

I thought about what I had witnessed in Ethiopia and how that compared with what most of us experience in the United States. We've never seen anything like it—we're so sheltered; our lives are so easy. If we're thirsty, we turn on a faucet and drink clean water. Our food is plentiful and good and healthful. We're well protected from danger. We have freedoms galore. So we don't understand disasters such as I witnessed in Ethiopia. We don't know of the need for our help. We don't know what to do.

In the past, when I returned from a trip to the third world and told friends what I had seen, they couldn't believe my stories, even though what I had seen during those trips had been nothing like the devastation I had witnessed this week. *How protected we are in America,* I thought. *How well-off we are.*

Contemplating my friend's question, I remembered learning that there are at least two thousand verses in the Bible that deal with the hungry, the sick, the poor, and the oppressed. No biblical instruction is clearer or repeated more often than our responsibility to "the least of these," as Jesus said (see Matthew 25:34–40).

I realized that helping people in need was how I was to bring God into my workplace, in a way that was right and clear and pure and not self-aggrandizing or hypocritical. This was how my life in Congress was to matter. I would travel among "the least of these," witnessing their needs, bringing those needs to the attention of my colleagues in Congress, my constituents in Dayton, and as many other people as I could—and work to have those needs addressed.

The relief workers at Alamata had taught me that I didn't have to solve every problem in the world. I just had to try to solve those I could.

Some years later, I had the great privilege of meeting Mother Teresa herself. I asked her how we could hope to solve the problems of the hungry, the sick, the poor, and the oppressed since there is such an overwhelming number of them. She replied, "You do the thing that's in front of you."

The lesson I took from her answer is this: If all of us did what was in front of us, think of how many problems we would solve. If each of us would take care of a neighbor, sit and talk with someone who is lonely, or feed someone who is hungry, think of what a better world this would be.

That, of course, is what Mother Teresa's missionaries were doing in Alamata in 1984. That's what I have been trying to do since I witnessed their example. In these two decades, I've seen many horrible things in front of me. I've also seen many good people working to make these horrible things better.

I'm writing this book to put these things in front of you.

CHAPTER 2

BROTHERS BEYOND POLITICS

Succeeding by Finding Common Ground

$\star$ $\star$ $\star$

When I returned from Ethiopia, I asked my good friend Frank Wolf to travel there too. "You must see what's going on there," I told him. "I won't be able to help them unless I have a partner, and I need you to be my partner."

So Frank quickly hopped a plane to Africa. He came back and joined my campaign to assist the starving Ethiopians. It was one of countless efforts we have made together on behalf of the hungry, the oppressed, and the poor—"the least of these"—over the last two decades.

At a quick glance, Frank and I would appear to be unlikely partners. He's a Republican U.S. representative from the South (Virginia). I'm a Democrat from the Midwest. When we cast our votes on the floor of the House, we disagreed almost all of the time. But we agree on some issues, and we've chosen to focus on those agreements. We have learned that if you concentrate on what unites you instead of what divides you, there's nearly no limit to what you can accomplish.

Our journey to personal friendship and political partnership began when a mutual friend asked me to join a prayer and Bible study group with Frank and two other House members, Dan Coats of Indiana and Bob McEwen, whose Ohio congressional district adjoined mine. We met once a week in one of our congressional offices, read Scripture, discussed it, and prayed. All that was fine. But we also talked about politics—a great deal of the time. As the only

Democrat in a group with three conservative Republicans, I didn't find that part so fine at all. After a couple of months, I finally told them I was going to stop attending the meetings for a while.

"I came to these meetings because I wanted spiritual growth," I explained. "I wanted to understand God better. I didn't want to sit around and talk about politics. We're in Congress. We talk about politics all day long. What makes this meeting any different from anything else going on up here? Guys, I need to take a break."

I didn't say, "I quit." But in my mind I was cutting it off, because it wasn't working for me. We weren't focused enough on God, the Bible, and prayer. We weren't really getting to know one another. So I drifted away. Bob and Dan remained my friends throughout our congressional careers, but this particular prayer group just didn't work.

Awhile later, our mutual friend came back to me and said, "Why don't just you and Frank get together? Take it easy. Try to get to know each other. Maybe take a trip somewhere together."

We both were leery of trying this again. Growing up in America, you're taught by society that to be successful, to be a leader, you have to be an island. You can't be vulnerable to others. You can't let people really get to know you, because they'll discover your weaknesses. And if they know your weaknesses, they'll take advantage of you.

This is an especially natural tendency for politicians. If I'm a Democrat, I can't be vulnerable to Republicans, because if they get to know me, they'll take advantage of me, and they might beat me in the next campaign. And I'll be really careful around Democrats who might run against me sometime in the future.

As a young politician, I learned to be partisan, to support my party no matter what, to be rough, to be sharp with my words, to be leery of developing personal relationships with people on the other side. But over time, I also observed that extreme partisanship often fails, leaving legislation unapproved, problems unsolved. Deep inside, I didn't feel good about my extremely partisan conduct, and I knew the American people didn't like it at all. (And the atmosphere in Washington was a lot milder back then than it is now.) Frank was having similar thoughts. He and I knew we shared faith. So we decided to make another attempt at fellowship.

I told Frank why I had left the original prayer group, so we agreed we wouldn't discuss politics. Instead, we prayed and discussed Scripture. We talked about our families, how we met our wives, what we did before we entered Congress. As the months passed, we began to let ourselves be vulnerable to each other, and I began to like him very much. When you each become vulnerable, you start to trust, your friendship can grow, and you can begin to do some really important things.

We took our first trip together in 1985 to Romania, which was ruled by Communist dictator Nicolae Ceaşescu. We were asked to make the trip by Christian Solidarity International, a Switzerland-based human rights organization concerned about the suppression of religion in Romania. It became a profound experience for Frank and me because it combined several matters of great importance to both of us—faith, human rights, and public policy. Frank's daughter Virginia; my wife, Janet; and Republican Representative Chris Smith of New Jersey traveled with us. We saw horrendous religious persecution and inspiring faith (which I describe in detail in chapter 5).

Traveling together, praying together, and witnessing dark oppression as well as bright faith deepened our relationship. We didn't talk about the partisan politics that divided us. We talked about the common challenge in front of us—how to promote religious freedom in Romania. When we returned to Washington, we launched a campaign to end the oppression in Romania and to provide encouragement to the Romanian activists who were fighting for freedom. I'm convinced our efforts made a modest contribution to the eventual fall of the Ceauşescu regime and the development of democracy there.

Traveling together, working together on important issues like human rights, creates a bond. You begin to trust each other. Then all the partisan baloney starts to fall away. Differences that seemed so consequential lose their significance. Frank and I disagreed on the vast majority of issues that came to Congress—taxes, appropriations, gun control, military spending, labor policy, various foreign policy matters, even the details of subjects about which we shared an overall agreement. We simply put them aside in our personal relationship and worked together on the issues on which we did agree, such as hunger, human rights, abortion, and family issues.

Over the years, we took half a dozen trips together to places such as Sierra

Leone, Benin, Afghanistan, Pakistan, the Balkans, and other regions in Europe and the United States. We worked to prevent international trade in diamonds that financed wars in Africa, to expose and prohibit slavery that was still being practiced in parts of the third world, to combat genocide in Sudan, to immunize children, to feed the hungry, to minimize abortion, and to teach others what we had learned about the value of fellowship and cooperation across divides.

During this time, Frank became my best friend in Congress. Our relationship has become my model for dealing with others. Focusing on issues of common concern has enabled me to work with and develop rewarding friendships with people who are both more conservative and more liberal than I am on many issues, but who share my passion for serving "the least of these" in some way. It also has empowered me to seek cooperation on specific projects from some highly unlikely partners, including even some people who are notorious for truly evil conduct.

A sort of mirror image of my relationship with Frank is my friendship with Al Franken, the comedian and liberal political advocate. Al and I don't share the same faith. (He's Jewish.) We don't see eye to eye on some social issues, such as same-sex marriage and abortion. You won't find me mimicking his fondness for telling off-color jokes and salting his public speaking and writing with vulgar language. But Al is firmly committed to assisting the disadvantaged, he's a strong supporter of efforts to end hunger, and he provided deep comfort to my family during our darkest personal hours.

In August 1992, our eleven-year-old son, Matt, was diagnosed with leukemia. After chemotherapy and radiation treatments failed to cure him, he spent months at New York's Memorial Sloan-Kettering Cancer Center being prepared for a bone-marrow transplant, which he received in November 1994. While Matt was there, a good friend of mine met Al, told him about my family, and said he should befriend us.

One day, Al telephoned, introduced himself, and asked if he could come visit us at the hospital. I said sure, and he came to meet us. I thought, *This is an amazing thing. Here's this guy from* Saturday Night Live, *a real celebrity, and he just came over to cheer up my son.* Then he asked if he could come back the next weekend and bring a friend. I said, "Sure. Who is it?" And he said, "Chris Farley."

So the next weekend, Al Franken and Chris Farley—two *Saturday Night Live* TV stars—came to the hospital to entertain Matt. Other people in the ward wanted to meet them, too, so Al and Chris went around entertaining everybody. They were hilarious. They were wonderful. Matt loved it. And that's how our relationship started.

Later, Al and I got to talking about hunger. I described what I had seen at some of the places I'd visited and also told him a bit about what I was doing to try to make things better. He seemed quite interested, so I suggested he take a look at the Bowery Mission Transitional Center in New York.

The center is remarkably successful at helping homeless men with drug or alcohol problems get back on their feet. It's also a great example of a faith-based organization operating with government support, in this case from New York City's Department of Homeless Services. It was run at the time by Bobby Polito, who later headed the second President Bush's Center for Faith-Based and Community Initiatives. Men live at the center for six to nine months while making the transition to a healthy life. While there, they receive counseling, job training, and other assistance. The center says that fewer than 10 percent of its graduates fall back into addiction.

After he visited the center, Al told me he was impressed by its effectiveness. I then asked him if he'd like to help in my work by joining the board of the Congressional Hunger Center, which I had founded in 1993 as an organization related to but independent of Congress. He agreed, and he's been active in the center ever since.

I've learned not only that people can work together across differences but also that everyone has special talents they can contribute to a cause. Not only can our differences be overcome, but our diversity gives us strength. In this case, Al is a celebrity and a marvelous comedian. He entertains at Hunger Center fund-raising events. In 2004, as a contestant on the "Celebrity *Jeopardy*" television program, he announced that the center was his favorite charity and told the national TV audience a bit about our work. He then went on to win $50,000 for us. On the political side, he came to Dayton and campaigned for Al Gore during the 2000 presidential campaign because I asked him to.

Even more important to my family, Al has become an exceptionally supportive friend. Throughout Matt's difficult illness and then after his death in

1996, Al would call to cheer and comfort us. He also made moving remarks at Matt's funeral. Nothing can be more devastating to a parent than the death of a child, and nothing can take away the pain totally. But Janet and I will always be grateful for the solace Al offered to us.

Another celebrity who has worked with me over many years is Martin Sheen, who is most famous recently for portraying President Josiah Bartlet in *The West Wing* television series. Like me, he was born and reared in Dayton (as Ramón Estévez; Martin Sheen is a stage name). Unlike me, Martin is a Roman Catholic. But his faith is real and deep and of great consequence to him, as mine is to me, and we have an identical understanding of God's admonition that we are to serve the poor.

Martin has been involved in many demonstrations on behalf of the hungry, the homeless, and the poor. In 2001 he helped Frank's and my diamonds campaign by cutting a television ad that was broadcast on NBC at the end of a *West Wing* episode. He came back to our common hometown—which he regularly visits, quietly, to see family—to campaign for my reelection to Congress.

Cal Thomas, the conservative media commentator, and his wife, Ray, fasted and prayed for Matt during his illness and have become close friends. Another conservative, John Nakamura, a retired farmer and former agriculture adviser to Republican governors in California, became my constant traveling companion.

I met John through a prayer breakfast I led in Washington for about fifteen years. Those who attended were a wonderfully eclectic collection of folks from around the Washington area—black, white, Asian, rich, poor, ministers, local politicians, some members of Congress, even some homeless people. Participation in the group made John and me friends, though not close friends. We developed a stronger friendship as a result of a chance encounter in South Korea in the mid-1990s.

I had just come out of North Korea, had met with some people in South Korea, and was feeling frustrated and depressed. As I explain in detail in a later chapter, enormous numbers of North Koreans were dying in a famine. Because of the North Korean government's repression of its people, threats to peace, and isolation from the free world, I couldn't drum up support for significant aid from the United States or from our allies in Asia. I believed that God had commanded us to feed the hungry, no matter where they lived. I had just spent time with innocent people, including children, who were severely hungry and at risk of death. But even my friends and some religious leaders questioned why I wanted to help this enemy. John happened to be in South Korea with a friend, and I ran into them. And I poured out my heart.

"John," I said, "I can't do this work anymore. I try to work with these ministers, who supposedly are men of God, and they won't help me feed the hungry. My own government thinks I'm crazy. I want to feed these people, but it seems nobody wants to help. I can't do this alone. I've got to have somebody with me. Frank has been with me on some trips, but he can't go everywhere with me."

John thought about what I said. Then he replied, "I want to be your partner. I will go on these trips with you, and I will support you, and I will pray with you."

Since then, John has traveled all over the world with me. He even moved to Rome and continued to travel with me during my term as ambassador. His agricultural background made him a perfect partner for addressing hunger. His fellowship strengthened me and enabled me to continue my work, even through difficult times such as those I experienced while trying to help people in North Korea. The Bible says that as iron sharpens iron, one person sharpens another (Proverbs 27:17). And Jesus said he would be present whenever two or more are gathered in his name (Matthew 18:20). I have found both to be true.

Another thing I have found to be true is that if you ask, you often will receive. Perhaps more remarkable than the relationships I've just described are the times I've received cooperation from some of the most feared and reviled individuals on the planet.

In November 2004, for example, I found myself standing in the desert in Libya, as Libyan trucks, piled high with bags labeled "USA," disappeared into the sandy distance on their way to Chad, to feed hungry refugees from the civil war in Sudan. The desert scene caused me to imagine I was playing a part in *Lawrence of Arabia*. The political reality that Libya had joined the United States in a humanitarian mission was nearly impossible to believe.

Libya had been our enemy. Our State Department had declared it a state sponsor of terrorism, and that designation remains in effect as I write this. Libyans had been implicated in the 1988 terrorist bombing of Pan Am Flight 103 over Lockerbie, Scotland, which killed 259 passengers and crew members—including 189 Americans—and 11 Scots on the ground. The United Nations had imposed sanctions.

In recent years, however, Libyan leader Mu'ammar al-Gadhafi had begun to take steps to join the civilized world. In 1999 he gave up two Libyans charged in the Pan Am bombing, and they were tried by a Scottish court. In 2003 the Libyan government accepted responsibility for the actions of the bombers, agreed to pay compensation to the victims' families, and renounced terrorism. The government paid compensation to victims of other terrorist acts that Libyans had perpetrated. Libya promised to dispose of its weapons of mass destruction and to end certain missile programs, and it began to cooperate with international agencies to implement those pledges. As a result, UN sanctions were lifted in September 2003, and the United States government was pondering whether to alter its view of this North African nation. I had been following these developments, and I began to wonder if we could use al-Gadhafi's image-enhancement campaign to solve a difficult problem we faced in the Darfur region of neighboring Sudan.

I had visited Sudan several times, both as a congressman and since I had become the United States ambassador to the United Nations food and agricultural agencies in Rome in 2002. Sudan—especially Darfur—is the site of some of the most horrific atrocities I've ever seen.

As a man of faith, I'm especially troubled by atrocities committed in the name of religion. Sudan's civil war, which has raged for most of the last fifty years, is, to a great extent—though not entirely—a product of religious conflict between the Muslim north and a south peopled by Christians and believers of several indigenous faiths. This is a place where great evil is done in God's name. The never-ending warfare has taken a tremendous toll, especially in the south. The fighting has created more than four million refugees and killed more than two million.

The conflict complicates relief efforts, and so does the weather. Supplies for Darfur—a landlocked area in Sudan's west—must be trucked twelve hundred to fifteen hundred miles from Port Sudan on the Red Sea or from the port of Douala in Cameroon on the Atlantic Ocean. During the rainy season—April through October throughout most of Sudan and longer in the south—the roads (where there are roads) can become impassable, and relief agencies routinely lose vehicles in flash floods.

During a briefing at World Food Program headquarters in Rome, I learned that a superior route could be taken through Libya, a route through an area with better roads and less rain. I broached the idea with State Department officials in Washington. Then I phoned Libya's ambassador to Italy and asked to talk with him.

Meeting in the ambassador's office, I explained the problem. "If we can ship food through your country," I said, "we can take it into Chad, which has refugees from Darfur, and we can take it into Darfur when the other routes are closed. It can be a third route to keep the food flowing."

He seemed open to the idea. Negotiations began. And in July 2004 the United States, the European Commission, the World Food Program, and Libya concluded an agreement that allows such shipments to occur into 2014. The first convoy of trucks left the Libyan port of Benghazi on the Mediterranean Sea in mid-August and arrived at the Oure Cassoni refugee camp in eastern Chad three weeks later. It carried food donated by Switzerland to feed 165,000 Sudanese refugees in Chad. The first U.S. food arrived at Benghazi in early November, three weeks after shipping out of New Orleans. I was able to meet that shipment when it arrived at Al Kufrah, an ancient trading post on the edge of the Sahara Desert. It was an awesome sight.

At Al Kufrah, Libya's asphalt roads end in sand, and the convoy drove off into the stark desert. The 350 trucks hauled 6,500 metric tons of sorghum, cornmeal, lentils, vegetable oil, and a corn-soy blend—enough to feed two hundred thousand refugees for more than two months, all in containers stamped plainly with the initials "USA." Each truck carried a driver, a mechanic, and a goat, in addition to the relief supplies. From the Mediterranean to the refugee camps in Chad, the convoy would drive seventeen hundred miles, mostly through desert. At the dinner break during each grueling day of desert travel, the travelers would slaughter goats to provide the meat for their meals. The trucks were Libyan. The drivers and mechanics were from Chad and Sudan. The food came from the United States. The whole process was coordinated by the World Food Program.

I flew to Al Kufrah on a Libyan airplane to represent the United States at this landmark occasion and to meet with Libyan and World Food Program officials who also came to witness the event. For lunch, we sat around eating dates and other fruits and chatting. The Libyans said they had never met an American before. And that underscored how remarkable this situation was.

It had started simply, in a phone call to a former—possibly current—enemy, with a request for help in a humanitarian cause. This cause was nonpartisan, nonpolitical, nonideological, and important to humankind. *If we can help hundreds of thousands of people by getting the OK from somebody who was an enemy and still may be an enemy, and we don't have to compromise anything,* I thought, *why wouldn't we do it?*

I had learned that such an approach could succeed a decade and a half earlier when Frank Wolf and I coaxed U.S. and Soviet leaders to cooperate in fending off starvation in Ethiopia. It was considered a significant event at the time, coming as it did at the end of the Cold War.

Ethiopia was still suffering from drought, famine, and civil war. Rebels in the northern regions of Tigray and Eritrea were making significant military progress against the troops of the central Communist government, which was still headed by Mengistu Haile Mariam. Because of the war, relief supplies could not be delivered into areas where some five million people were at immediate risk of death. The Eritrean People's Liberation Front, which was seeking independence from the central government, had targeted the port of Massawa, the main entry point for food and other emergency supplies. Food unloaded there had been destroyed. The fighting threatened to keep the port closed for months.

In a carryover from the Cold War, the Soviet Union provided weapons to the Mengistu government. The United States and other countries had sent food to Ethiopia and had more in the pipeline that was being blocked by the war. Both publicly and privately, Frank and I asked the first President Bush and Soviet president Mikhail Gorbachev to join forces in pressuring all parties in the war to observe a "food truce." We wrote newspaper opinion pieces, appealed to representatives of the Ethiopian factions, and met with U.S. and USSR officials.

"Now is the time for an eleventh-hour humanitarian offensive, led by President Bush, joined by President Gorbachev and working through the U.N. Security Council," we wrote on the *Washington Post*'s op-ed page on February 21, 1990, for instance. Our article continued:

Nothing less than a full-scale international assault against hunger in Ethiopia, led by the superpowers and the United Nations, has a chance of success.

A "food truce," through which white-flagged relief convoys would cross battle lines to reach civilians, could be arranged.

Most of the results of the thaw in the Cold War have thus far been political: new governments in Czechoslovakia and Poland, steps toward German reunification and an end to one-party rule in the Soviet Union. Here is the chance—indeed the duty—to use the warming of relations for humanitarian ends.

President Bush and President Gorbachev answered our pleas. The result was a cease-fire that permitted delivery of food and other relief supplies to those Ethiopians who were facing starvation in the absence of aid.

This hopeful approach to enemies, whether past or present, led me to request a simple humanitarian act by a man who at this writing remains a fugitive from the United Nations war crimes tribunal at The Hague.

In July 1995 I traveled to the Balkans, where ethnic groups were fighting to control pieces of what once had been Yugoslavia. In Croatia I marveled at the beauty of the Adriatic coast and its role as a low-cost Riviera during peacetime. In Sarajevo, which had so successfully hosted the 1984 Winter Olympics, I encountered some of the worst horrors of this civil war.

Yugoslavia, a multiethnic state that Communist dictator Josip Tito held together for decades after World War II, slowly deteriorated following his death in 1980, then crumbled along both ethnic and religious fault lines in the 1990s. When I arrived, Bosnians, mostly Muslims, were under siege in Sarajevo, surrounded by Bosnian Serbs, mostly Christians, who were led by Radovan Karadzic, the president of the Serbian Democratic Party. Sarajevo desperately needed food, but UN relief caravans were blocked by Serb military forces. The people were desperate, emotional, and in shock. I saw many women, children, and older people but no men, young or old. They were either fighting or hiding in the forest.

Karadzic, who already stood accused of war crimes, had representatives in Washington. So before I left the United States, I told them I'd like to meet him during my trip. Our State Department asked me not to do so. "I'm not going over there to make policy," I replied. "We have a humanitarian crisis, and I want to ask him to lift his snipers to at least let some food into Sarajevo." The Serb representatives said Karadzic would see me.

Even though Karadzic's headquarters were just a few miles from Sarajevo in the mountain town of Pale, we couldn't travel safely between Muslim- and Serb-controlled territory in Bosnia. So I and three aides who were traveling with me had to fly from Sarajevo to Rome, then to Frankfort and on to Belgrade, the capital of Serbia. From there we drove six hours to Pale.

We arrived in the evening, exhausted from having slept only about an hour each of the previous four days. Karadzic immediately summoned us into his headquarters for talks. He knew about my faith, said he was a believer, and suggested that we pray. He offered us dinner. We talked from about seven or eight o'clock that night to two or three o'clock the next morning.

I stressed the humanitarian purpose of my trip. "The whole world looks on you as a monster," I told him, "and I can see you're worried about that." He said he wasn't the monster the world thought he was and that he wanted to change his image. "If that's the case," I replied, "do something. Don't just talk." Pointing out the convoy of food trucks that couldn't pass his military lines, I continued, "Allow this convoy to get into Sarajevo."

"Yeah," he said finally, "I'll take care of it."

This conversation occurred during the time that Bosnian Serbs were committing perhaps the worst atrocities seen in Europe since World War II. Mimicking the Nazi attacks on Jews, Bosnian Serb troops seized the small spa town of Srebrenica, rounded up the men and boys, and slaughtered more than seven thousand of them. Yet here was their leader, calmly sitting and talking with me, promising to do good.

Two years later Frank and I traveled to Bled, Slovenia, a beautiful little town by a lake at the foothills of the Alps, where people from across the Balkans were meeting as part of a long-term effort to learn to live in peace. Frank and I told them how we reached across our political differences to work together. I also told them about my strange encounter with Karadzic.

Afterward, a man came up to tell me he had been in Sarajevo at that time. "All of a sudden," he said, "Karadzic let this big food convoy come in, and we never understood what happened."

These kinds of experiences make me particularly frustrated about the lack of civility and cooperation within our own politics and government. Frank and I weren't the only members of Congress to build a close working relationship across partisan lines. There are other small clusters of members who meet in regular prayer groups. The House hunger committee was a bipartisan enterprise from the moment Mickey Leland, an African-American Catholic Democrat from Texas; Benjamin Gilman, a white Jewish Republican from New York; and I led the effort to create it in 1983. After the committee was abolished a decade later (which I write about in detail in chapter 6), Frank, Missouri Republican Bill Emerson, and I created the Congressional Hunger Center to keep working on the issue. The center's board is cochaired by one member of Congress from each party.

Bipartisanship also defines the House and Senate hunger caucuses, less-formal successors to the House Select Committee on Hunger. Nebraska Republican Tom Osborne and Massachusetts Democrat Jim McGovern—who represent quintessential "red" and "blue" states—cochair the House caucus. The Senate caucus has four cochairs—Democrats Blanche Lincoln of Arkansas and Richard Durbin of Illinois, along with Republicans Gordon Smith of Oregon and Elizabeth Dole of North Carolina.

Osborne and McGovern are the prime House sponsors of the Hunger-Free Communities Act, a legislative proposal that has long been one of my goals. It would set the objective of cutting hunger in the United States in half by 2010 and ending it by 2015. Lincoln, Durbin, and Smith joined Indiana Republican Richard Lugar to introduce the bill in the Senate. Many legislators also work across party lines to represent the special interests of the communities or states that they share.

It's hard—almost impossible—to build close, personal friendships with people and then publicly attack them. I can't tell you how many times Frank and my other conservative Republican friends have leaped to my defense when I've been attacked unfairly from the right.

It is possible to disagree about issues; Frank and I disagree about most political matters. But you can have debate—civil debate—on the many issues you disagree about while still working together to achieve the few goals you share. It's difficult to work together on the few common goals, however, if your many debates turn vicious, bitter, personal, and blindly partisan. Unfortunately, in recent years, this kind of debating has become common practice in Washington. And that's one major reason I'm happy that I decided to leave Congress after almost twenty-four years.

It's nearly unfathomable to me why our politicians are incapable of understanding the value of civility, friendship, and cooperation. If, to achieve a specific humanitarian goal, I can find common ground—however briefly—with the likes of Karadzic and al-Gadhafi, why in the world can't Republican and Democratic politicians in the United States find the common ground where they could solve our nation's very real problems? Why can't we all come together to answer our common summons to help the poor?

There are Republicans who refuse to work with Democrats and Democrats who refuse to work with Republicans. There are people of faith who refuse to work with people who don't have faith, Christians who refuse to work with non-Christians, even members of one Christian denomination who refuse to work with members of another Christian denomination.

I'll work with anyone who shares a common goal with me. As a follower of Jesus, I would like my friends to believe, and I hope that they will come to do so someday. But I'm not going to refuse to work with them because they don't share my beliefs. And I'm not going to try to push my faith down their throats. It's really up to them, not me, to figure out their relationship with God.

What I can do is follow Jesus's command to serve the poor. My friends and others who work with me see what I do and come to understand why. Often people ask me why I work to help people in need. It's remarkable how many people have become believers after getting involved in humanitarian work.

The poet Edgar Guest once wrote, "I'd rather see a sermon than hear one." I've carried that sentiment with me ever since I first heard it. It follows Jesus's instruction to "let your light shine before others, so that they may see your good works and give glory to your Father in heaven" (Matthew 5:16).

CHAPTER 3

WALKING WITH MOTHER TERESA

Doing What's in Front of Her

✸ ✸ ✸

T he first time I met Mother Teresa, she took my left hand in hers and said, "I want you to always remember something." Then she used her other hand to deliberately fold each of my five outstretched fingers, one by one, into my palm. With each fold, she said a word: "For . . . the . . . least . . . of . . . these. I want you to always think of this. For the least of these." She also said, "Pray and keep a pure heart and be humble." Then she took me with her on her rounds through Calcutta and taught me a great deal more about how one should go about serving the poor.

The overarching lessons I have learned from my travels are that there is need in the world far beyond most affluent Westerners' comprehension and also that there is hope. No place did I find that hope shining more brightly than in the dark slums of this great Indian city. The world has heard of Mother Teresa's accomplishments, but you cannot fully understand the power of her faith and love unless you were able to accompany her in her work. And were you, like me, able to do that, your life was forever changed.

I was with a small group of believers from the United States. We began our day at the Missionaries of Charity compound in Calcutta, which was made up of plain wood-and-concrete structures where the missionaries lived and carried out some of their work, and where Mother Teresa kept a modest office. Everything there was clean and simple—drab, even. Mother Teresa's office had off-white walls, as I recall, and a simple table with simple wooden chairs. The compound included a small hospital, facilities for caring for quite a few orphans, and a little chapel. The plainness of Mother Teresa's living and working conditions struck me, because it contrasted so dramatically with the grandeur of her mission and the enormity of her accomplishments.

We accompanied Mother Teresa first to a hospice. It was a single large room in which sixty to seventy poor Indians who were very sick lay on simple iron beds and waited to die. It was primitive, but it was clean and peaceful and comfortable. The missionaries washed the patients, fed them, talked with them, touched them. Normally, dying brings great sadness. But with Mother Teresa and her missionaries, death was peaceful and pure because of all the love that filled the room.

We next went to a home for severely retarded children. The facility resembled the hospice—another big room, spartan, devoid of color, and housing maybe sixty children, most of them lying or sitting on iron beds. These places would not meet U.S. standards for health-care, educational, or service facilities.

No one wanted these kids. They were so mentally disabled that it appeared they were unaware of their surroundings. Many were physically disabled as well. The room was filled with incoherent babbling. Yet when Mother Teresa walked in, these kids lit up as if the sun had suddenly come indoors. They all started to yell and expressed excitement in wonderful ways. She walked through the room, hugging each child. When she touched them, they glowed. It was amazing to see how much she loved them and how much they loved her in return.

She had the same effect at an orphanage we visited, although there the children were healthy and energetic. When we walked in, the kids—fifty to sixty of them, ages three to about nine—jumped on us as if they were playful puppies. They hopped up and down, hung on us, touched us, wanted to play with us. So we sat on the bare floor in this large playroom, which contained only a few toys, all of them fairly simple, and played with these kids, joked with them, touched them. They craved attention, craved physical contact, and they responded to Mother Teresa's love.

I noticed throughout the day that wherever we went, she touched everyone she was working with. She made everybody feel her love. And the poorest, the sickest, the most physically and mentally disabled responded with joy and love. Touching the poorest and the sickest is not an easy thing to do. They often don't look good. They don't smell good. They may not be clean. They may be slobbering or defecating in their beds or throwing up. Sometimes flies swarm around them. You wonder what germs are swarming as well, what illnesses they have that they might pass on to you. Yet none of that seemed to bother Mother Teresa. And the touching, the hugging, the demonstration of love seemed to be perhaps the most important thing she did.

I thought of this later, far away in Kinshasa, the capital of the Democratic Republic of the Congo, where my friend John Nakamura and I noticed the streets seemed to be filled with children who appeared to be homeless. They were not, it turned out, orphans of war or of AIDS. Rather, they had been declared "witches" by self-proclaimed religious doctors and had been banished by their families, left to fend for themselves despite their young age.

We were able to visit a Catholic organization that was taking care of some of these kids. The children told us how they had been kicked out of their homes, had to scratch for subsistence on the streets, had no family to love them. As we prepared to leave, we hugged them, and these outcast children responded powerfully. They hugged us back tightly. They cried and cried. They kept holding on to us. They didn't want to let us go. Their reaction drove into my soul just how important love and touch are to people who are deprived of both.

Another time I thought back to Mother Teresa's example was when I met Sister Surupa at a clean but primitive hospital run by the Missionaries of Charity in Port-au-Prince, Haiti. The hospital, which cared for AIDS and tuberculosis patients, had few of the modern medical tools we take for granted, and five patients had died just the day before.

"What care can you hope to give in this place?" I asked her.

"Loving care is what we give," she replied.

With Mother Teresa in Calcutta, we visited orphans, lepers, polio victims, the handicapped, the mentally ill, the mentally disabled, and the dying. Every time she entered a room, everyone in the room came alive. If you just looked at her, you would hardly call her a beautiful woman. Physically, she was not an imposing figure. She probably was less than five feet tall. But she had a beauty and an aura about her that I have never seen in anyone else.

The facilities we visited that day were scattered around the city. Sometimes we drove from one site to another. Sometimes we walked. At one point while we were walking, I became overwhelmed by the vastness of the sickness and poverty that surrounded us. There were masses and masses of people living practically on top of one another in the crowded slums. It was swelteringly hot. Open sewage flowed along the street. Cattle and other livestock wandered everywhere. People were lying on the streets, living on the streets. It didn't smell good. I thought not only of the squalor that surrounded me at that moment but of the horrors I had seen in my earlier travels. At that kind of moment, you wonder if there's really any way you can make a difference that truly matters.

Someone asked Mother Teresa, "Don't you think what you do is kind of a drop in the bucket?"

And she answered, "No, it's a drop in the ocean. But if I didn't do it, it would be one less drop."

"But," I said, "the problems of the world are so vast. How can you possibly hope to solve them?"

"You do the thing that's in front of you," she replied. And that was the most important lesson she taught me.

"A man asked me that question many years ago when I first started my ministry on the streets," she told me. "There was a woman very sick in front of me, like that man you're looking at right there," she continued, pointing to a man lying on the ground in front of us. "Her face was bitten by ants and rats. I took care of her and loved her, and that's how I started my ministry on the streets."

We can't all go to Calcutta to help these people. But if we each do the thing on our street—do the thing that's in front of us—we will make the world a much better place.

Mother Teresa's story is a personal example of both doing what's in front of you and reaching across many boundaries. She was born in 1910 in Macedonia, of Albanian descent. At age eighteen she joined the Loreto Sisters in Ireland. They sent her to teach high school in Calcutta.

What she saw in front of her there were the poor, the sick, the homeless, and the orphans, living on the streets of the slums with no one to help them. So in 1948 she left the school to work with the poorest of the poor. In 1950 she founded the Missionaries of Charity to love and care for people whom no one else would help in a country that is 80 percent Hindu, 13 percent Muslim, and 2 percent Christian. She learned Bengali, the major local language, and became a citizen of India. She said her goal was to "make a Hindu a better

Hindu, a Muslim a better Muslim, and a Christian a better Christian." In its early years, the order opened a hospice, then an orphanage, then a home for lepers, then other facilities to care for the neediest.

Originally a small band of nuns, the Missionaries later added brothers as well. Today Mother Teresa's movement has grown to encompass forty-five hundred sisters, five hundred brothers, and countless thousands of volunteers who serve "the least of these" in more than one hundred countries. To the original homes for the dying, orphans, and lepers have been added numerous facilities for unwed pregnant women, AIDS patients, the mentally and physically disabled, the destitute, and others. In the words of Pope John Paul II, "A great host of people—of all beliefs and none—have become involved in this work of love which has spread throughout the world."[1] Beyond even that, Mother Teresa has inspired countless others to do their own good works, even if they don't have the all-consuming commitment that she demonstrated and that her missionaries still exhibit.

She had no power, as power is traditionally measured. She didn't hold a government office. She didn't own a gigantic business. In fact, this humble woman owned nothing except a few changes of the plain Indian clothing she wore everywhere. She lived among the poor. She spent most of her time with the poor. Yet she influenced the entire planet.

The importance of her work was recognized when she was awarded the 1979 Nobel Peace Prize, which she accepted with the request that the usual gala banquet be canceled and the money saved be donated to the poor. In her acceptance speech—and wearing her simple Indian sari—she asked her audience to "find the poor here, right in your own home, first, and begin love there, and find out about your next-door neighbor—do you know who they are?"

Her profound impact on the world was dramatically demonstrated at her death in 1997. President Clinton summed up her life perfectly by describing her "ministry of action—of passion and compassion." He said, "She led by serving and showed us the stunning power of simple humility."[2] The president asked First Lady Hillary Clinton to lead the United States delegation to the funeral, and she invited me to attend. It was an extraordinary sight.

The government of this overwhelmingly Hindu country declared national days of mourning and honored the diminutive Roman Catholic nun with a state funeral, a tribute reserved for high government officials with only one previous exception—Mahatma Gandhi in 1948. In the days leading up to the funeral, tens of thousands of ordinary Indians made their way to St. Thomas Catholic Church, where her body was laid out. The body was carried from the church to the funeral site—an indoor sports arena that could accommodate thirteen thousand people—by the same military gun carriage used in the funeral processions for Gandhi and Jawaharlal Nehru, India's first prime minister. In Mother Teresa's case, the procession featured nuns from her order and representatives of the poor, the disabled, the sick, the orphaned, and the homeless. Dignitaries from several dozen countries attended the funeral mass, including presidents, prime ministers, first ladies, and three queens.

Cardinal Angelo Sodano, the Vatican secretary of state and the pope's personal representative, presided. The choir sang hymns in several languages. The prayers and eulogies were both multilingual and multifaith, including contributions from Catholics and Protestants as well as a Hindu, a Muslim, a Buddhist, a Sikh, and a Zoroastrian.

The media revealed her broad appeal when obtaining comments from both dignitaries and people on the streets.

"At a time when humankind is being increasingly driven by selfish motive, she gave selflessly to those whom society has forsaken and forgotten," said Atal Bihari Vajpayee, head of India's leading Hindu nationalist political party.

Manik Chatterjee, caretaker of a Hindu temple, said, "It is not possible in one hundred thousand people to replace her. What she did, no one else can do."

"When someone is so good," said a Muslim named Mohammad Qasim Ali, "their religion does not matter. She was a foreigner, not even an Indian. But people thought she was one of us."

"Crossing the frontiers of religious and ethnic differences," said Cardinal Sodano during the funeral mass, "she has taught the world this lesson: it is more blessed to give than to receive."

It's amazing how many extremely effective humanitarian organizations sprang to life when one person or one small group of people did what was in front of them. The Grameen Bank—along with the global microcredit movement it has inspired—can trace its origin to economics professor Muhammad Yunus's visit to a poor village in Bangladesh in 1976, for example.

"I became involved in the poverty issue not as a policymaker or a researcher," Yunus recalled three decades later. "I became involved because poverty was all around me."[3]

As an economist, Yunus said, he dealt with theories about international trade and billions of dollars in business transactions. But while confronting the poverty in front of him, he "wanted to find something specific to do to help another human being just to get by another day with a little more ease than the previous day."[4]

In the village of Jobra, near Chittagong University, where he headed the Economics Department, Yunus met Sufiya Begum, a twenty-one-year-old mother of three who made bamboo stools. Raw materials for each stool cost just twenty-two cents. But she had no capital. So she had to borrow, either from moneylenders who charged interest as high as 10 percent a week, or from a middleman who would buy each completed stool for just two cents more than she paid for the raw materials. If she could borrow at a reasonable rate—as established businesses and middle-class individuals can—she could earn enough to save and improve her economic standing, Yunus reasoned.

Yunus and a student surveyed the village and identified forty-one other craftspeople who were in the same straits as Begum. The professor then reached into his pocket and loaned the forty-two people a grand total of $27. All of the borrowers repaid their loans. And Yunus thought he had discovered the secret to helping the underprivileged lift themselves out of poverty.

With a great deal of difficulty, he convinced a bank to devote $300 to such loans. But the bank required him to guarantee each loan, and the lending procedures were extremely cumbersome. In late 1977 another bank, the Agriculture Bank, put $30,000 into starting an experimental Grameen Branch in the village. In mid-1979 a consortium of national banks enabled Yunus to open another two dozen branches, and he took a leave of absence from the university to oversee the enterprise. With support from the national banks and the Ford Foundation, expansion continued into the early 1980s. In 1983 Grameen became an independent bank. In 1998 it stopped relying on grants from donors to pay some of its expenses.

Grameen, which means "village" in the Bangla language, breaks many established rules of banking. In addition to lending to the poorest of the poor, it demands no collateral and does not require borrowers to sign legal instruments. The bank doesn't threaten borrowers with court action if they fail to repay—and it doesn't have to. Its default rate is a remarkably low 1 percent.[5]

Because traditional Bangladesh banks seldom loan to women, Yunus set a goal of giving women half of Grameen's loans. Later he determined that a loan to a woman tended to bring more benefit to the family than a loan to a man. Now women comprise 96 percent of the bank's borrowers.[6]

The bank also counts about forty-five thousand beggars among its borrowers. Their loans are interest-free and long-term, so the installment repayments can be small. They often finance something as basic as a blanket or mosquito netting. Beggar borrowers aren't required to stop begging but are encouraged to seek other ways to generate income. Grameen has loaned beggars close to $1 million, and half of those loans have been repaid.[7]

Today Grameen fields a staff of about 14,000 to operate more than 1,500 branches. Since its inception, it has loaned nearly $5 billion, including a projected $550 million in 2005 alone.

From its beginning of loaning tiny sums to village craftspeople, Grameen now offers a wide range of loans, such as loans for housing, education, and even high technology. More than 600,000 houses have been built with Grameen loans that average just $210. More than 6,000 students have received higher-education loans, including about 100 who attend medical school and nearly 200 who are studying to become engineers. About 140,000 have borrowed to purchase mobile telephones, which they use to bring phone service to villages that have never had it before. These so-called telephone ladies sell the use of their phones to villagers one call at a time. Some earn $300 to $400 a month in a country with an annual per capita income of about $450. The bank has placed a special emphasis on putting phones in the hands of beggars to provide an alternative source of income. A majority of Grameen's borrowers have lifted their families above Bangladesh's poverty line. Borrowers own 94 percent of the bank's equity. The bank pays 8.5 to 12 percent interest on deposits that total about $400 million.[8]

Yunus has been a tireless campaigner for microcredit, spreading the concept far beyond Bangladesh. He was not the first person to consider the value of tiny loans, nor the only person to try to put the idea into effect, writes David Bornstein in his book *How to Change the World.* But Yunus "worked without pause to institutionalize and market his idea," Bornstein says. And "it is unlikely that micro credit would have grown into a major global movement without Yunus' vision, single-mindedness, persuasiveness and energy."[9]

Yunus certainly influenced me.

Just as I believe we have the capability to banish hunger from the world, Yunus believes we can eradicate poverty, "if we want to."[10] And he makes a powerful argument that his approach—acknowledging a responsibility to the poor but helping them to become entrepreneurs rather than simply giving them relief—can bring people together across ideological gaps.

"You may be a revolutionary, a liberal or a conservative—you may be young, or you may be old—but we can all work together on this one issue," Yunus writes in his autobiography, *Banker to the Poor.*[11] "It's amazing," he said later. "Whether I'm talking to Republicans or Democrats, Labor parties or Conservative parties or Christian Democrats, they all agree on supporting this idea."[12]

I travel around the third world to learn about poor people's needs and ways that I and my wealthy country can help. But in Bangladesh, from Yunus, I learned how his knowledge could help the poor in America.

Yunus talks of the need to "reverse the age-old vicious circle of low income, low saving and low investment," replacing it with a "virtuous circle of low income, credit, investment, more income, more savings, more investment, more income."[13] There's no reason that approach can't work in the United States, home to the most entrepreneurial people in the world.

There are plenty of poor Americans who have the ability to run a small business, who are willing to work hard, but who never get a chance. In fact, many are already doing it; we just don't recognize it and don't give them the small support they would need to grow. I'm talking about women who operate informal day-care centers by taking neighbors' children into their homes, men who push a mower along sidewalks while carrying a can of gasoline and looking for lawns to cut, others with buckets and sponges who offer to wash neighbors' cars.

After learning from Yunus, I introduced or cosponsored several pieces of legislation that provided government support for microlending and changed welfare rules that penalized poor people who earned and saved while trying to improve their families' economic state. Ironically, we supported microenterprise abroad through our foreign aid programs before we encouraged it at home. And it works.

I met a woman in a small town in southeastern Ohio who used a microenterprise loan to start a car-wash business—not with large, expensive machinery but with a few people who wash autos with their hands. Stories like hers have been replicated across the country. A woman in Arkansas borrowed $475 to buy the used equipment she needed to open a beauty shop. A $650 loan enabled a woman in Nebraska to start a greenhouse and landscaping business.[14]

Yunus views "every single human being as a potential entrepreneur. I am totally convinced from my experience of working with poor people," he says, "that they can get themselves out of poverty if we give them the same or similar opportunities as we give to others. These millions of small people with their millions of small pursuits can add up to create the biggest development wonder."[15]

I have met many people like Muhammad Yunus during my travels—people who did what was in front of them. Many have eased one person's misery through a simple act of kindness. Some, such as Yunus and Mother Teresa herself, began by reaching out to a few people, then went on to change a large chunk of the world.

I try to pass their lessons on whenever and wherever I can. While I was ambassador in Rome, I often was asked to speak to Italian audiences about my travels. Once, at a high school in the southern region of Molise, the students asked me what they could do to make the world better.

"We can't all go to Calcutta," I replied. "Look around you. Your next-door neighbor maybe just lost her mother, or maybe her father just lost his job, or maybe there's somebody sick in their family. They need your attention. They need you to love them. They need you to talk to them. They need a friend.

"Maybe there's an outcast here in the school whom everybody looks down upon or makes fun of. First, don't do that. Then be his friend.

"Somebody around here needs a helping hand, and you can provide it, and oftentimes it's a very simple thing. Just look around you, and you'll see it. If you don't see it, then ask. If you just scratch the surface a little bit, you'll find something that you can do. And after a while, if you see problems that are bigger, and you're a leader, and you have the passion, you'll figure out a way to bring in other people and raise money and do whatever needs to be done to address whatever problems you want to address."

CHAPTER 4

ALL IN THE FAMILY

Doing What's in Front of Us

★ ★ ★

One of the most heart-wrenching and heartwarming scenes I've ever witnessed during my travels took place at an orphanage in Uganda, where my wife, Janet, and I had taken our kids to volunteer. An enormous proportion of the orphans were HIV-positive or had AIDS. Some were visibly sick. The orphanage was so poor that the babies didn't wear diapers. Our daughter, Jyl, then fifteen years old, was holding, hugging, and playing with a baby who had both thrown up and urinated on her. Yet Jyl was acting as if nothing was wrong. "They just need somebody to love them," she told us.

Because I have been a congressman and an ambassador, my humanitarian activities have received a lot of public attention. Not so well known is the fact that Janet and Jyl are dedicated humanitarian workers as well, as was our son, Matt, until he died of leukemia at age fifteen in 1996. Jyl, in fact, earned a master's degree at Asbury Seminary in Kentucky and is setting out on a career of service to the poor.

Janet has been involved in these activities as long as I have. They've always been discussed at the family dinner table. From the time Jyl and Matt were old enough to understand, we made a concerted effort to expose them to the needy and to teach them the importance of helping those who are less well-off than we are.

Because of Janet's and my activities, we were able to take our kids to some pretty exotic places and to help them experience firsthand the extremes of

45

privilege and deprivation. At home and abroad, they met high-ranking government officials and people with great wealth, including some who use their government positions or their affluence to help the poor. They also met people who had nothing. We took them to work at soup kitchens and in church service projects near our home in Washington, something any parent can—and, I think, should—do. From time to time, I took them with me in my work around Dayton.

If you introduce children to these things, let them see hunger and poverty in the flesh, let them share in helping, then serving the poor becomes part of their lives. After a few of these experiences, Matt and Jyl never questioned why I would leave home to travel overseas or help in a homeless program or work for the hungry. In fact, they would ask to come along.

Jyl says her first memories of being exposed to these issues flow from conversations around the family dinner table or in front of the television. Just as I had been involved in humanitarian activities before my trip to Ethiopia, she had begun responding to family discussions of hunger and poverty when she was about six years old, before she had any direct experiences with severe poverty. She did so by donating some of her allowance to good causes. Also, as it had on me, my trip to Ethiopia had a profound effect on her.

Jyl didn't accompany me to Ethiopia then, of course. She was just eight years old. But I talked a lot about my experiences there after I returned. I can become quite emotional, and I guess I often teared up when discussing what I saw. Jyl noticed my emotion and grasped the fact that doing something to help was important to me. When appeals for aid to Ethiopia would come on the television while we were watching some show together, they moved her too. Later she said that my reactions to these things showed her clearly that God was working in my life.

One of the first times we involved our children in a hunger project was in 1985, when Jyl was nine and Matt was four. I organized a forty-hour fast in Dayton to raise funds for antihunger programs there and overseas (an event I write about in detail in chapter 7). Although the kids didn't fast, Janet and I took them to Dayton with us so they could experience the occasion. I also took Matt with me to visit a Dayton homeless shelter.

In Washington, where my family and I spent most of our time, we all worked in local soup kitchens. I helped start a gleaning program, through which a Maryland farmer let us collect unharvested produce from his fields for delivery to Washington food programs. Matt and Jyl often would go with me to pick fruit there. They also helped in our church's project to deliver food to the poor, many of whom were refugees of civil war in El Salvador. One year, we spent Christmas in Florida and agreed we each would give the family a present that couldn't be purchased. Janet's gift was to take us all to work in a soup kitchen on Christmas Day. As we did these things, the children would ask questions, mostly about why people had to be so poor, why they couldn't find a place to live, why they were so poorly dressed, why some acted strangely.

We also just tried to be good friends and neighbors. We'd take food to neighbors who were sick, visit with friends who were lonely or troubled. We tried to show Matt and Jyl that they just had to look around themselves to find good deeds that needed doing. And they did.

Once, while visiting a home for the elderly, Jyl noticed that many residents seemed lonely and didn't receive many visitors. So she started to regularly visit two women who shared a room. She'd sit with them on weekends. They'd tell her stories about their lives and ask her what she was up to.

Janet wanted to expose our children to the widest possible array of experiences, so she arranged in 1987 for Jyl to spend some time with an extraordinary Ethiopian couple who then were living in Fort Wayne, Indiana. Marta Gabre-Tsadick had been the first woman appointed to the Ethiopian Senate during the reign of Emperor Haile Selassie, and she had served as the hostess at his palace. When Communist rebels overthrew Selassie in 1974 and began executing members of Selassie's family and government, Marta fled with her husband, Demeke Tekle-Wold. They ended up as refugees in Indiana, where, with the Reverend Charles Dickinson and his wife, they founded Project Mercy in 1977.

Initially, Project Mercy provided emergency relief and relocation assistance to African refugees. Following the collapse of Ethiopia's Communist dictatorship in the early 1990s, Marta and Demeke returned to their homeland and have built at the village of Yetebon one of the most effective private relief and development projects I've seen anywhere in the world.

Jyl considers meeting Marta and Demeke to be one of the formative experiences of her life. Our families remain close to this day. We visit them from time to time when we are in Africa, and they have visited us in Washington and Rome. Jyl has described Marta and Demeke as being like grandparents to her.

At age eleven, Jyl learned something of hunger, poverty, and oppression by talking with Marta, Demeke, and other Ethiopians who had found refuge in Indiana at that time. Perhaps more important, she learned about and became comfortable in an alien culture, even though it had been transplanted temporarily to the American Midwest. Understanding the society of the people who need help is essential for anyone trying to succeed in humanitarian ventures.

The trip to Uganda, however, was what really set Jyl on the path to a lifetime of service to the poor. Again, the idea was Janet's—another part of her plan to expose our children to the very best and the very worst aspects of life on earth. "We have only a limited amount of time to teach our children," Janet said. Knowing and helping the poor had become a regular part of their lives at home. Living with Marta and Demeke had enlightened Jyl. But Janet believed it was important for both Jyl and Matt to witness firsthand the severe deprivation that exists in the third world.

Janet and the kids spent a month in Uganda, the first two weeks without me because Congress was in session. Jyl noted the staggering contrasts she experienced that month. We stayed in a diplomatic residence in the capital of Kampala. We were driven to the orphanage in a car provided by President Yoweri Museveni. At the orphanage, we worked with children who had nothing—not even, Janet pointed out, parents.

The orphanage was poor. The children slept on the floor. There wasn't enough money to put the babies in diapers. They had few toys to play with. Matt, who was ten at the time, played soccer and other games with the older children. It was wonderful to see the orphans' faces light up with smiles when they saw him coming. Jyl, who was fifteen, devoted herself to the babies. When she sat on the floor, they would crawl all over her. One by one, she'd hold them, hug them—love them. We had other activities planned for our stay in Kampala, but Jyl returned to the orphanage nearly every day.

The experience was "a shock," she recalled many years later. "I was just completely overwhelmed that there were people who lived like this. I don't know if I'd even met an orphan up to that point. It just broke my heart, and it changed my life forever."

About the babies with AIDS, she said, "I'd just hug them and hold them, because I thought, *How many people are here to hold these children? And who knows how many days they have till they die?* I thought, *I don't want to do anything else with my life but to do this kind of thing.* I think that's when I really started to believe this is what life is about. It's about caring for one another, reaching out to those who are hurting, and giving from my own surplus."

Because Matt was younger, this trip didn't have such a profound effect on him. But as he got older, he developed a tremendous heart for people who were hurting. And these people sensed it when he was around them. I'll never forget one time, after he got sick, when I visited a homeless shelter in Dayton. His illness had been reported in the Dayton media, and even the homeless were aware of it. Several homeless men came up to me and asked, "How's your son? How's he doing? We think about him all the time." And I thought to myself, *These guys slept out in the cold weather on the street last night. They don't know where their next meal is coming from. And here they are worrying about me and my son.* When you care for the hungry, care for the poor, they return it to you in the way they can.

Jyl recently decided to earn a master's degree in theology to help her prepare for a career in ministering to "the least of these." As part of her studies, she wrote a paper titled "A Biblical Theology of Mission to the Poor." To write it, she searched for all of the biblical references to the poor and struggled to understand their meaning.

"It is interesting," she writes, "that Jesus did not solve the problems of poverty everywhere he went. Jesus often repeated that this burden was on us all." Later in the paper, she concludes that "giving to and caring for the poor should bring joy and purpose into people's lives. The fruit of God's love in our lives, and our response to it, is love. The response to forgiveness is forgiveness. The response to mercy is mercy. I hope to continue to educate people on the need for mission and care for the poor. I believe that holistic mission is caring for both the material and spiritual needs of others."

In addition to studying, Jyl is helping her fellow students get involved in humanitarian action. She's compiling a list of activities students could undertake in the local community. She counsels students about finding the activities that would be best for them. She helped to found a local chapter of Amnesty International to join the fight for human rights around the world. She participates in letter-writing campaigns to public officials in the United States and abroad. She volunteers in political campaigns.

Janet and I, of course, are thrilled by the path she is taking—by the fact that she wants her life to count and that she wants to serve the poor. I'm sure this desire is rooted in what she experienced in Dayton and Washington and Africa. It's no coincidence that Frank Wolf's children have chosen similar paths.

When Frank and I traveled through Romania during the dark days of the Nicolae Ceauşescu regime, Frank brought his daughter Virginia along. It was a horrifying and inspiring trip, as I describe in chapter 5. Virginia, then a college student, experienced everything we did. She even joined us in speaking to congregations in Romanian churches that the Communist government was trying to destroy. Shortly after returning from Romania, Frank took his entire family on a trip through Europe, including behind the then-still-hanging Iron Curtain in East Germany. He called it a true eye-opener.

Frank's children worked in their church's mission projects. As in our house, Frank's humanitarian activities—and the reasons for them—were topics of conversation around the family dinner table. When you follow the message of the Bible, Frank says, you feed the hungry, clothe the naked, free the oppressed, and serve the poor.

Frank both talked the talk and walked the walk, as they say, and his children have too. Among them, they have worked with the poor and homeless in Washington, taught in Romania and Honduras, worked with the needy in Bolivia, and helped to start Christian schools in Washington, D.C., and Princeton, New Jersey.

Janet and I are well aware that Jyl did not have a typical childhood—and neither did Frank's children, for that matter. Jyl has seen great luxury and abject poverty up close. And she experienced the horrible personal tragedy of losing her younger brother to cancer when he was just fifteen years old.

We're not rich. Despite what many voters think, most members of Congress aren't rich. We are better off than most Americans, however, as are most federal legislators. And many rich people participate in politics. So Jyl has been in the homes of some very wealthy families and ridden in their limousines. She has attended functions at the White House and met presidents. She has accompanied me to national political conventions. She has traveled in two dozen countries. She has visited Janet and me in our diplomatic residence just inside the ancient wall in Rome.

She also has worked in grassroots politics, especially in my campaigns— riding in parades, knocking on doors. She attended public schools where she was in the racial minority. She has done humanitarian work in places of extreme poverty, as I've already told.

Jyl's desire to serve grew from these diverse experiences. But any parent can inspire a child to want to do good in any community—you don't have to go to Africa. Your kids learn by your example.

You don't force your kids to participate in a humanitarian project. You talk about serving others. You live it. You do it. You take them along with you when you do it. They need to see it with their own eyes. They need to feel it. They need to try to understand the shoes the other person is walking around in.

You can take them with you to work in a homeless shelter or food bank in any American city. They can serve by visiting shut-ins down the street. If they feel this service is genuine in your life, it will stay with them throughout their lives. They'll never forget.

As Jyl said recently, "My parents could have talked to me till they turned blue, and I wouldn't have really been that interested in their preaching about helping people. I had to see it in their lives—I had to see them really having a heart for what they're doing—or I would have thought they were just talking."

I have known and learned about many families that have made a difference in people's lives in small but important ways. Sometimes people's initially modest efforts end up accomplishing great things beyond their wildest imaginations.

Often I discover the parents in these families have been doing good works since their own childhoods. Their parents encouraged them to serve, and they pass this ethic on to their own children. When this happens, it's likely to continue for generations.

Geri Critchley remembers how she and her eight siblings were reared in Forestville, Connecticut, by devout Roman Catholic parents who "gave their lives to the community and to the church." The family put on "fairs for the missions" every year, selling popcorn, setting up games in their yard, and hosting a dance in the garage. When she was little, Geri didn't understand exactly what the funds they raised were used for. She just knew they gave the money to their priest and he did something good with it.

Her father was a wonderful singer, she recalls, and he organized his large family into a singing group. Each Christmas Eve, they would carol for shut-ins.

As a young adult, Geri joined the Peace Corps and served in Somalia. Later, when she began rearing her own children, it was natural for her to introduce them to service at an early age.

"It was a conscious decision on my part to make sure they understand that it's in the giving that you receive," Geri explains. "But I didn't really 'teach' them. It just sort of permeated our lives."

Geri and her children held lawn sales to raise funds for Special Olympics. They delivered food to a soup kitchen. She took them along on her various service projects. She sent them to Catholic schools that emphasize service as an integral part of education. As they got older, they took on projects of their own.

When he was about fourteen, her son, Otis Plioplys, spent a summer building and upgrading houses on an Indian reservation. Later, as an avid golfer, he became inspired by Tiger Woods's efforts to bring golf to inner-city children. So Otis began teaching golf to kids on an urban course in Washington. His high school—Georgetown Prep, in a Washington suburb—has its own golf course, and he arranged for his inner-city golfers to spend a day playing there. He recruited fellow Georgetown Prep golf team members to be golf tutors for the day. He convinced some restaurants to donate food for the event. He did what was in front of him. Or as Geri puts it, "he used what he knew to do something good."

As juniors at Stone Ridge School, not far from Georgetown Prep, Geri's daughter, Hiliary Plioplys, and her best friend, Elizabeth Schroth, organized a group they called People for Peace. The purpose, Hiliary said, was to increase their fellow students' awareness of world affairs and "to do something ourselves to make a difference."

During school meetings, they made announcements about current events. They staged a volunteer fair to alert students to opportunities for public service in their community. They held bake sales and a grilled-cheese-sandwich sale to raise money for various causes. They ran a "shoe drive," collecting used but good shoes to donate to an organization in Kenya. Then they met Tom Ehr, executive director of War Child USA, an international relief and development organization that focuses its work on children affected by war.

He told the girls his organization had raised funds to purchase relief supplies for children in refugee camps in Kosovo, a war-torn section of the Balkans. War Child didn't have enough money to hire trucks to deliver the supplies, however.

"He told us," Hiliary recalls, "'If you want to make a difference, it's about $5,500 per truck, and we need about four. Any effort you guys make to raise money for that would be great.'

"I thought, *This is crazy! $5,500—that's insane!*"

But Hiliary and Elizabeth took on the challenge. They made announcements at school, posted signs, and encouraged students to donate and to solicit contributions from their families and friends. They convinced school administrators to set aside a day when students wouldn't have to wear Stone Ridge uniforms if they brought in a contribution for the Kosovo drive. They received donations from alumni. They got their message through to even the youngest students.

"One little girl at the school had a bake sale to raise money and donated something like $23.75, and she was so happy to be able to donate it," Hiliary says. Another child, a kindergartner says raised funds with a lemonade stand.

One of Hiliary's mother's friends told Hiliary about putting her young granddaughter to sleep the night before dress-down day. "We were praying for everyone in the family," her mother's friend related, "and my granddaughter added 'those little children in Kosovo.' I asked her, 'How did you know about that?' And she said, 'Oh, at my school everybody knows that. We learned about it, and we're dressing down tomorrow, and I'm going to bring in my fifty cents.'"

When dress-down day arrived and People for Peace finished adding up the contributions from the school's eight hundred students, "everybody completely flipped," Hiliary says. More than $16,000 was collected that day. When all the contributions came in, they totaled $17,500. War Child used the money to hire three trucks and purchase additional supplies.

The project's spectacular success focused attention on Hiliary's little group. People for Peace received grants to stage a rally promoting service on Youth Service Day. The event, held at Washington's John F. Kennedy Center for the Performing Arts, drew students from around the Washington area and featured a performance by famed folksinger and social activist Peter Yarrow. The kids designed T-shirts displaying a statement attributed to Mahatma Gandhi: "You must be the change you wish to see in the world."

Hiliary was asked to speak at a conference of the National Society of Fundraising Executives (now called the Association of Fundraising Professionals). There she met Doris Buffett, investor Warren Buffett's sister, whose Sunshine Lady Foundation underwrites charitable giving by young philanthropists. Each year, Hiliary can donate up to $10,000 of the foundation's assets to nonprofit organizations that meet the foundation's funding criteria.

Now a college graduate, Hiliary plans to attend medical school in preparation for a career in international public health. In doing so, she follows both parents' leads. Her father, A. V. Plioplys, is a physician. Her mother is her inspiration to serve the less fortunate.

"I think, in my innate character, because of my upbringing, is the belief that you should, through your career and your everyday actions, leave the world a better place than when you came into it," Hiliary explained. "I'm not happy unless I'm helping other people in some way. It's part of who I am. My mom's that way, and I'm that way."

Not far from Hiliary's home, Maureen and Greg Gannon have instilled their commitment to service in their four daughters. Maureen (known as Mo) and Greg actually met while doing good. After graduating from the University of Notre Dame, Greg reinvigorated a tutoring program for disadvantaged children in Washington. A recent graduate of Villanova University, Mo was a volunteer tutor in the program, called Higher Achievement.

The program runs after-school tutoring and summer classes for middle school students in poor neighborhoods who have the motivation to succeed. The goal is to get them admitted to the Washington area's best public and private high schools and then into college. More than three-quarters of the participants have been admitted to what Higher Achievement defines as "quality high schools." Nearly all of the participants—not just those attending the best high schools—have gone on to higher education.

Now the development director of the Catholic archdiocese of Washington, Greg remains on the Higher Achievement board. He, Mo, and their children have been active in various volunteer programs.

When oldest daughter, Katie, was about nine years old and youngest daughter, Margy, was about three, Greg organized a gleaning project at the family's church, Blessed Sacrament. Over the years, he expanded the effort by recruiting students and families from nearby Catholic schools. Participants would attend Sunday morning Mass, then travel to a farm. They'd glean for about two hours, break for a potluck picnic, then glean for a few more hours. Even Margy participated from the beginning.

Later Greg started a canned-food drive, again beginning at Blessed Sacrament, then expanding. Each year, he recruited volunteers, divided the Blessed Sacrament parish into sections, and assigned responsibility for canvassing each area. The Gannon family stapled flyers promoting the drive to grocery bags and distributed the bags to the volunteers. The flyers asked the neighbors to fill each bag with canned food and to leave it on the doorstep. The volunteers delivered the bags to homes in their neighborhood. A week from the date of the grocery bag distribution, drivers accompanied by children returned to collect the bags. The volunteers then gathered at the church for a snack and to count the cans.

After the drive became established within the Blessed Sacrament parish, Greg started recruiting families who lived outside the parish but whose children were enrolled in the Blessed Sacrament School. He asked them to solicit contributions in their neighborhoods. The drive became so popular that neighbors started looking forward to it. Many would make a special shopping trip and leave several full bags at the door. Greg has relinquished leadership of the drive to others, but it has become an institution in the community, now collecting more than forty thousand cans of food a year.

"I think as human beings we have the obligation to sort of look after the people who are less fortunate than we are, that we have a responsibility to give back," Mo said. "If you're lucky enough to have more than you need, you should share some of that.

"I think you can really instill that in your kids. I think our kids are pretty aware of how much they have and how much a lot of other people don't have."

The Gannon girls' actions prove Mo's point. All four participated in additional volunteer programs while living at home and continued to do so after they left for college. Katie worked in soup kitchens while a student at Villanova University in Philadelphia and tutored Mexican immigrants in English when she lived in San Diego for three years after graduation. Margy, a freshman at McDaniel College in Maryland, worked with Special Olympics while in high school. Megan is active in her sorority's service programs at Miami University of Ohio. Colleen volunteered in tutoring and mentoring programs while an undergraduate at Notre Dame. She's now teaching in a rural Catholic school in Louisiana while working toward a master's degree in education at Notre Dame during the summer.

Katie, who now teaches at Saint John's College High School in Washington, says the girls' volunteer work today can be traced to those childhood experiences collecting cans and gleaning food that otherwise would go to waste.

"When we would go through those fields to glean, it seemed there was enough to feed thousands of people and it was all going to spoil," she says. "It gave you some insight into how wasteful our country is in general, and that there are people who have so much and people who have so little.

"It motivates you more than parents just saying, 'Eat your dinner, because there are kids who don't have enough to eat.'"

CHAPTER 5

ROMANIA

Faith Deposes Might

Romania in 1985 was one of the most oppressed places on earth, yet its government enjoyed relatively friendly relations with ours. This was one of the great contradictions of the Cold War years, when the United States government—proclaiming the cause of freedom—would prop up dictators simply because they weren't Communists. In Romania, our position was even more convoluted, because dictator Nicolae Ceauşescu *was* a Communist. By distancing himself from the Soviet Union, he had been able to convince successive U.S. administrations that it was somehow in our best interest for him to remain in power.

The illegitimacy of that position was apparent from the moment my traveling party landed in Bucharest, the Romanian capital, at the end of June 1985. Despite the supposed amity between the U.S. and Romanian governments, U.S. diplomats immediately hustled us from the airport to a so-called bubble room in the American embassy.

A bubble room is equipped with all sorts of antispying technology to prevent eavesdropping on meetings that take place there. Once safely inside, we were warned of Romania's robust intelligence apparatus. We were cautioned to assume that everything we did, wherever we were, including in our bedrooms, would be *observed*, not just listened to. The Romanian government had one of the worst human rights records in the world, the embassy personnel informed us. The secret police terrified the people. Romanians also had to endure the lowest standard of living in Europe outside Albania.

I had traveled through desperately poor places before—places much poorer than Romania, in fact—so seeing the poverty of the Romanian people would not be a unique experience for me. But this was my first trip among people subject to such severe political repression. And the fact that I had brought Janet along on this trip made the situation that much more disturbing.

Christian Solidarity International, a Switzerland-based human rights organization, had asked me—along with Frank Wolf and Republican Representative Chris Smith of New Jersey—to investigate reports of religious persecution in Romania. Frank's daughter Virginia and Janet accompanied us. Very quickly we all observed the truth of the briefing at the embassy. The oppression was so heavy, you could actually feel it. We were stopped and questioned wherever we went. We constantly spotted signs that we were being followed. We had numerous meetings with people who we thought would help us to understand the real state of affairs there but who played down or denied the extent of repression—because they were afraid. We sat in meetings—sometimes at meal tables—with government officials who baldly lied to us when we had incontrovertible evidence of the contrary truth. We also witnessed great bravery and inspiring faith among Romanians who held fast to their convictions and refused to stop worshiping in the manner they believed they should, despite the fierce government pressure.

We had been told that the government's campaign against religion included deploying bulldozers to destroy churches, so we visited one. It looked like the ancient ruins around Rome. Half of the church had been reduced to rubble. Some walls still stood in the other half, and they supported a partial roof. Members of the church had spread tarps across what was left of that roof so they could continue to worship there. It resembled the damage found in the aftermath of war. This damage had been done not by some enemy nation's bombs, however, but by this country's own government-directed heavy machinery.

This congregation demonstrated great faith, resiliency, and defiance by resuming services in their church. I have never seen spirit more beautiful and powerful than I witnessed there. It showed me that spirit often is strongest among the oppressed, because it's the only place they can turn for support. I saw it in all four churches we visited during this trip.

On the way to the town of Aradia, for instance, we were delayed. Government officials went to the church we were supposed to visit and told the people waiting for us that we weren't coming. They then ordered the people to disperse. But the people stayed. And when we arrived, the pews were filled, the aisles were packed, and many other people stood outside. They were singing hymns in hearty voices when we walked in. The love and faith in that building were so strong they seemed to have a physical presence.

The government tried to block all of our church visits. Secret Service officers went to places we planned to explore and warned the people not to meet with us. We knew the people at all four churches faced imprisonment, beatings, and torture for displaying their faith in public. Many of them had relatives or friends who had been imprisoned or killed or who had simply disappeared. Yet each church overflowed with worshipers, many of them wearing tattered gray clothing. We were told people had stood for as long as three hours awaiting our arrival. When we finally did show up, they hung on to every word when we spoke to them. And we listened intently to their tales of oppression.

They told us of priests and pastors who had become informants for the secret police and of the way that people in all walks of life spied on one another. They showed us toilet paper that had been manufactured from Bibles confiscated by the government. Ceauşescu, it seemed, viewed the Bible as an extremely dangerous instrument in the hands of the faithful, so he made Bibles hard to come by.

Janet carried a beautiful new Bible into the churches we visited. At one church, the people expressed great admiration for it. Because Bibles were denied them, they had an enormous hunger for the written Word of God. Janet responded to their desire by giving the Bible to them. I later thought about what a wonderful act of kindness she had performed and regretted that I hadn't done the same.

At each church, people would touch us and hug us to express love as well as gratitude for the fact that we had come to be with them. Some kissed us on both cheeks in the European way. Many wept. Some stuffed pieces of paper into our hands or pockets. When I got to my hotel room that night, I counted a dozen of those notes, and so did Frank and Chris. They were pleas for us to help specific individuals—a husband who had been in jail for ten years, for instance, or a neighbor who was missing. The universal message was this: "Let the outside world know what is happening here."

As we traveled from city to city, we stopped once at a farm that had been described as one of the more prosperous in the region. The farm family served us a very simple meal outside. They and their neighbors were warm, emotional, and generous. I noticed that the farm had no indoor plumbing and that the house and tools seemed quite primitive. It looked much like I imagine farms in the United States looked around the end of the nineteenth century.

I got the impression the family had gone to a great deal of trouble—and what for them would have been great expense—to obtain the ingredients needed to prepare the meal. You could tell this was the best they could offer and they were proud of what they had prepared. We did everything we could to show gratitude and pleasure. But to our American tastes, the food was terrible. It seemed they had thrown everything they had into a soup, including things most Americans would never eat. I remember specifically noticing chicken feet floating in the broth.

Some of us became sick and had to run to the outhouse, which consisted only of a shelter around a hole in the ground. There was no seat. There was no toilet paper.

I didn't expect the common people in a repressive Communist country would possess many luxuries, but I was surprised to find this extent of poverty anywhere in Europe. We were told Romania had run so short of power the previous winter that gas was turned off across the country in late January. The elite's offices and houses remained heated, but I wondered how many of the poor had died from the cold.

Our visits brought great hope and encouragement to the people we met. They lived in a closed society that tried to shut them off from the rest of the world. They couldn't know whether people outside cared about them and were trying to help. They drew strength from us, because we showed that others were thinking about them and endeavoring to set them free. At the same time, we drew strength—and a mandate—from them. Seeing their plight made us realize that they were depending on us to assist and that we had to come to their aid. Witnessing their courage and faith inspired us. I felt honored to meet them, share their vision, and be asked to help.

We also drew inspiration from stories about people we didn't get to meet, especially Father Gheorghe Calciu, who spent more than two decades in Romanian prisons for opposing Communist oppression. Ceauşescu released Father Calciu from jail before our trip to Romania but kept him under house arrest, so we weren't able to visit him. We finally met him later, after he was allowed to leave Romania. He visited us on Capitol Hill to thank us for our efforts to free him and for our work on behalf of the Romanian people, and to urge us to press on.

Calciu first was arrested for protesting Communist rule in Romania after World War II. He was released sixteen years later, in 1964, and was ordained as a Romanian Orthodox priest in 1972. He was imprisoned again in 1979 after delivering a series of sermons the preceding year that denounced religious persecution.

Calciu vexed the government during his second imprisonment because he had become well known not only in Romania but around the world. His very imprisonment called attention to Ceauşescu's repression. The government was afraid to let him go free, because he probably would resume his public protests. It feared that killing him might upset Romania's relations with the United States and other Western nations. U.S. and European citizens were conducting letter-writing campaigns to Western government officials, asking them to pressure the Romanian government to free Calciu. They also wrote to Ceauşescu himself to plead for Calciu's freedom.

When Calciu came to see us in Washington, he described what had happened inside the prison during his second incarceration. First, he said, he was tortured—beaten, deprived of food and drink, stripped of all but tattered clothes, and confined to a windowless, unheated cell. He was allowed to sleep six hours a night on a wooden board. Then the board would be removed, and he was left with only the concrete floor to stand, sit, or lie on. The jailers subjected him to psychological pressures that were designed to break his will. They insulted him, his family, and his faith. They even urinated on him. He was given a pot to relieve himself in, and twice a day he was required to empty it in a restroom. While walking there, he would be hit and pushed. If he spilled anything, he had to clean it up with his bare hands. Always deprived of wine, often deprived of bread, he couldn't fully celebrate his church's Divine Liturgy (or Mass) on most Sundays.

When all this failed to cause Calciu to accept the legitimacy of Ceauşescu's policies, prison officials concocted a scheme to have the priest killed while deflecting the blame away from the government. They promised leniency to two hardened criminals in the prison if they would murder him. They then made the prisoners his cellmates.

The two criminals informed Calciu they planned to kill him. They forced him to stand for long periods, beat him, and required that he obtain their permission before eating, drinking, or using the chamber pot. Then, after about a month, they told him they had decided not to kill him. He asked for their permission to celebrate the Divine Liturgy with the bread and water they had in the cell. They agreed, and he was stunned when they knelt with him to pray. His faith was so strong that it turned these would-be killers away from murder and toward prayer.

Amazingly, after all his ordeals, Calciu had no bitterness toward those who had so mistreated him. He was not a large man, less than five and a half feet tall, relatively slight of build. When he came to visit us, he was wearing an orthodox priest's black cassock. His hair and beard were a mixture of white and gray. His face was warm, gentle, and joyful. His countenance was alive, hopeful, and at peace. I recognized the great faith that had sustained him for all those decades of persecution.

Before we left Romania, we met with several government officials and were stunned by their audacious lies. They were openly hostile, treating us as if we were enemies. They told us that Romanians enjoyed great religious freedom. They denied that some of the bulldozed churches ever existed, even though a number of them had stood for centuries. They asserted that other churches had been demolished because they violated building codes. They said those who alleged persecution were liars, that imprisoned Christians were murderers and thieves. Father Calciu, they charged, had been a Nazi. When we asked about reports that nearly twenty thousand Bibles had been turned into toilet paper—some of which we held in our hands—a foreign ministry official called it "a story manufactured by a Hungarian in Connecticut"!

We knew these words were false. And though these Romanian officials spoke with great firmness, you could see the dishonesty in their faces—especially in their eyes. The foreign minister, in particular, looked like a violent mobster. He was a burly man with a stern demeanor, and I thought he probably chewed nails for breakfast. The closed nature of these men's society was demonstrated when the trade minister mentioned he had "heard that" a Romanian ambassador had resigned—something we had learned two weeks earlier in the United States.

Romania's Ministry of Culture and Cults exercised substantial control over the Romanian Orthodox Church hierarchy and cowed leaders of other faiths through the force of fear. Before Father Calciu's imprisonment in 1978, for example, the Romanian Orthodox patriarch expelled him from the church because of his antigovernment sermons. A Romanian Orthodox archbishop told us that "there are no martyrs in the Romanian Orthodox Church." A Roman Catholic bishop admitted that "we're not living in a bed of roses." But, he added, "we are not being persecuted, or we would not be allowed to meet." We met a priest who had access to a printing press and asked if he would allow it to be used to print Bibles. He said no.

We felt both sadness and anger when we left the meetings with these church leaders. We understood that they had reason to be afraid. Still, we wished they had exhibited more courage, as had many rank-and-file clergy and believers.

In our meetings with government officials, we demanded more freedom for the Romanian people and the release of prisoners like Father Calciu. We gave them a paper, signed by all three of us, that put them on notice that we planned to take action in Congress if their human rights record didn't improve. If we didn't detect an increase in freedom, we would work to do away with Romania's Most Favored Nation status—a designation that eased the country's ability to sell its products in the United States, a benefit that every nation wanted. Romania's independence from the Soviet Union had won the designation. We believed Ceauşescu's clear record of oppression provided a reason to rescind it, an action that would cost Romanian exporters about $1 billion a year.

While we were inspired by the courageous demonstrations of faith we had witnessed in the churches we visited and in the stories we heard about brave dissidents like Father Calciu, Romania's repression beat down on us like a deadweight. When we returned to the United States, Frank, Chris, and I immediately sought news media coverage of the repression in Romania, and we got involved in letter-writing campaigns. We delivered one letter to Nicolae Gavrilescu, Romania's ambassador to the United States, demanding action on a dozen specific abuses of religion, including the detention of Father Calciu. Sixty-six of our House colleagues sent a letter to the Romanian government. Senate Majority Leader Bob Dole and our State Department also called for Ceauşescu to change his ways.

Calciu was freed shortly after our trip, and he took refuge in the United States. Ceauşescu did not respond directly to our demands, however, so in September we sent a follow-up telegram, which he also ignored. In October we introduced legislation to suspend Romania's Most Favored Nation status for six months, with reinstatement contingent on an increase in religious freedom and an improvement in the country's overall human rights record. Republicans Paul Trible of Virginia and William Armstrong of Colorado offered similar legislation in the Senate.

The road to passage of the legislation was hard. The Reagan administration and leaders of both parties in Congress opposed us. First, we were warned that attacking Romania would make it more difficult for the people living there. Frank and I took this argument seriously and contacted Romanians who had been imprisoned or tortured or had relatives killed. "It can't get any worse than it already is," they told us.

We testified before congressional committees in support of our resolution, and the committee members sympathized in public with our goals, praised our statements, and thanked us for our good work. In private, they repeated the arguments that successive administrations had made about Romania's importance to U.S. foreign policy.

"It's not as bad as you think it is," they said. "They're kind of distancing themselves from the Soviets. We have a chance to change them by cooperating with them. Sure, these are bad guys, but they aren't as bad as the really bad guys. This is an opportunity to put a crack in the Soviet Bloc. This is the wise, realistic approach, as opposed to your impractical idealism."

Some of these committee members thought they really understood Romania because they had visited there. But they had met with the government officials in Bucharest, been wined and dined and treated as the visiting dignitaries they were. They didn't travel to the places we did. They didn't visit bulldozed churches or poverty-stricken farms. They didn't hear common people tell their horror stories. Their "realistic" argument worked on the surface. But they never scratched below the surface to see what was really going on.

The fact is that I am a realist. I look at the world and see that the future belongs to freedom and democracy. I know it's not going to happen overnight, that it takes time to break the chains of oppression like those that were locked in Romania. But our policy in Romania—as in too many other parts of the world today—was penny-wise and pound-foolish. It focused on the short term and ignored the long run. "Don't rock the boat now," the leaders told us. "Don't worry about it now."

But the Romanian government was just as bad as, if not worse than, the Soviet Union when it came to oppressing its own people. By treating Ceauşescu as the rightful leader of Romania—by treating him even as a friend!—we were legitimizing him in the eyes of those who did his bidding, and we were dashing the hopes of those who longed for freedom.

Father Calciu noted after his release that while he was in prison in the 1980s, Ceauşescu "was traveling all over Europe, attending merry banquets offered him by presidents, kings, and queens. The triumphant reception of their president convinced the guards that Ceauşescu was esteemed in the free world and precious to Romania, and therefore, anyone who didn't accept his decisions had to be killed. And I was one of those people."[1]

I knew the people of Romania would seize control of their government in the long run—and, in fact, they did. And when that happens—in Romania and elsewhere—the people remember if we stood with their oppressors or if we worked for freedom.

I believe we should try our best to build peaceful relationships with all governments, regardless of whether we find them personally attractive. But we also can exert peaceful pressure for change. At the very least, we shouldn't reward countries for bad behavior. And we were rewarding Ceauşescu's Romania for very bad conduct.

Frank, Chris, and I—along with other representatives and senators who worked with us—grabbed some attention in the news media. But for a couple of years, the administration and leaders in Congress blocked our proposals at various stages of the legislative process. Nonetheless, we were winning the long-term battle for public and congressional opinion. By 1988 it became clear that we were going to succeed. Both the House and the Senate approved the six-month suspension of Romania's Most Favored Nation status. Before the legislation could take effect, Ceauşescu renounced the status on his own, complaining that the United States was meddling in Romania's internal affairs.

By then, those internal affairs weren't going so well for Ceauşescu. It seemed very appropriate that his government's religious persecution was what sparked the protests that led to the toppling of his regime.

In mid-December 1989, word got around the city of Timisoara that Ceauşescu's secret police were about to arrest and deport a Hungarian Reformed Church pastor named Laszlo Tokes. Like Father Calciu, Rev. Tokes had been an outspoken critic of the Communist regime, complaining about the suppression of religion and denouncing Ceauşescu from the pulpit. Also like Calciu, Tokes was disowned by church leaders who feared the government. They ordered him out of his church, and the police were sent to remove him when he refused to comply.

When police arrived, they encountered a growing crowd of Tokes supporters who had surrounded the church to protect him. At first, the demonstrators prayed and lit candles. Later, the confrontation between police and protesters turned violent. Word of the clashes spread quickly across the country, and soon anti- Ceauşescu crowds formed in Bucharest and other cities. As the number of demonstrators in the capital grew by the tens of thousands, soldiers joined the protesters in confronting the secret police. Within ten days, the government fell and Ceauşescu was executed. Our State Department estimated that fifteen hundred people died in this fast-moving revolution.

Later, both Tokes and Calciu explained how their faith supplied the guidance and strength they needed to confront their oppressors and how faith played an essential role in overthrowing the Ceauşescu regime.

"I think that 'protest' is the most important part of the word *Protestant*," Tokes said in an interview with the *Boston Globe*. "To protest against something and to protest for something, this is my tradition."[2]

In a speech to the Hungarian Reformed World Conference, Tokes said Ceauşescu "wanted to deprive us of God and alienate us from other people. It was like taking an ax and chopping at the roots of our communities." But, the pastor added, "as Reformists we can answer this with a truly Reformist saying: 'If God is with us, who can be against us?' Those who love God will come to no harm. That is the answer of the Word, an answer based on faith."[3]

Father Calciu related his experience in nearly the same way. Speaking to a conference of the Christian Relief Effort for the Emancipation of Dissidents, he described how he expected to be murdered by Ceauşescu's agents in prison:

> There were many of them. I was alone and defenseless. There was no law to prevent them from committing such a crime. There were no moral principles to stop them.
>
> I had faith. They had force. Then again, they had nothing, because they did not have God. I had the love and spiritual help of my fellow man, praying for me throughout the world. They had nothing but their hate. And because this conflict was a spiritual one, they were defeated, in spite of all the material power on their side.[4]

Our experiences while traveling in Romania and later working against the Ceauşescu regime solidified my relationship with Frank and confirmed the course of my human rights activism.

Frank, Chris, and I all learned that if you focus on an issue, join forces across partisan lines, and stay together, your effectiveness soars. We also learned that people in places like Romania in the 1980s depend on us to help them. It's a very lonely battle for them. And it can be a lonely battle for a member of Congress who takes on an issue like this. Constituents and other legislators will ask, "Why are you messing around with Romania? Nobody cares. How many Romanians live in your district?" But I believe a government is measured—a country is measured—by how we reach out to the poor, how we help the hurting, how we fight for the oppressed.

The other thing these experiences underscored is that what we did mattered. The oppressed of Romania took strength from knowing that people outside were working on their behalf. It was hard work, but we convinced our fellow legislators that the United States should not reward Ceauşescu for his evil deeds. And we discovered that even Ceauşescu knew what we were doing, and it angered him.

CHAPTER 6

THE FAST

Follow God, Lead by Example, and the People Will Respond

★ ★ ★

I n March 1993 I found myself burning with anger.

I had helped to create, and later chaired, the House Select Committee on Hunger. It had been the vehicle that empowered me to call public attention to the problems of hunger, poverty, and oppression at home and overseas. It enabled me to summon witnesses to hearings that caused Washington-based media to report about tragedies—such as famine in Africa, oppression in Haiti, and hunger on U.S. Indian reservations—they otherwise might have ignored. It financed my trips to trouble spots around the world, entitled me to useful support from the State Department, and increased the likelihood that foreign governments would cooperate with me. It provided me with a dedicated, expert staff who made me so much more effective in my work. It helped me convince other committees to consider legislation that the hunger committee devised but did not have the authority to bring before the full House for passage.

The *New York Times* had termed the hunger committee "the conscience of the Congress." We were widely credited with causing or contributing to a significant number of important accomplishments—establishing the office of the United Nations undersecretary for humanitarian affairs; convening a humanitarian summit among conflict- and poverty-stricken nations in the Horn of Africa; preserving threatened U.S. nutrition programs for poor women, infants, and children; expanding disaster-relief programs; funding child-survival activities; establishing programs to help welfare recipients start small businesses; and heightening public and government awareness of childhood immunization shortcomings, famines in various nations, hunger in poor U.S. communities, and other humanitarian challenges around the world.

And this wonderful committee was about to be taken away from me.

Even though Democrats comprised the House majority, a group of relatively young, conservative Republicans was growing in influence. Many citizens were responding favorably to these legislators' attacks on Congress itself as a bloated, wasteful, ineffective institution. Many Democratic lawmakers were running scared, fearful that we would lose the powers of the majority we had enjoyed for nearly forty consecutive years. (And, in fact, Republicans did take control of the House and the Senate in the elections of 1994.)

These Republicans had seized on the idea of making Congress more efficient by reducing the number of committees, and they started by taking aim at four "select" committees, including my hunger committee. The select committees were created to investigate and make recommendations about a specific topic. Unlike "standing" committees, the select committees did not have the authority to take legislation to the House floor. They did not oversee the budgets of any government agencies. They had relatively small staffs and relatively small budgets. (The hunger committee's budget was the smallest in the House.) And they didn't have rich and powerful constituencies that cared about their work, the way the agriculture industry cares about the Agriculture Committee or the defense industry cares about the Armed Services Committee.

My anger was compounded by the knowledge that the poor and the hungry don't speak with a loud voice on Capitol Hill or in political campaigns. They don't have a political action committee that makes big campaign contributions to influential legislators. They don't hire well-connected and well-paid lobbyists to advance their interests in Congress and the administration. House members would not pay a significant political price for killing off the hunger committee, and they could pretend they were striking a blow for efficiency and common sense by whittling down the size of the federal government.

I worked hard to convince my colleagues to save the hunger committee, but by March it was clear that I would lose. If the House did not vote to keep the select committees functioning by March 31, they would cease to exist. While I was able to gather support from 180 House members, I needed 218 for a majority. The leaders of my party—the majority party—could have kept the hunger committee in business to serve the poor. They could have helped me round up the votes. But Speaker Tom Foley said he would not even schedule a vote if I could not prove I would win. The Republicans had the Democratic leaders running scared, and the select committees were sacrificed so that Democrats could appear to be cutting wasteful spending.

I was heartbroken and irate. I no longer would be a chairman. I no longer would have this vehicle for doing the work that made my political life worthwhile. Since my first trip to Ethiopia nearly a decade before, I had used the committee to be a loud voice for the disadvantaged and the downtrodden. It was how I brought God into my workplace, obeying the many biblical admonitions to care for those in need. I grasped for a way to respond.

My first inclination was to search for a way to strike back, to get revenge, to find a means for releasing my anger. I considered quitting Congress. I conjured up hateful images of the institution that had been my home for fourteen years. I now saw it as a viper pit, filled with hypocrites who cared about nothing but their own reelections. I tried everything I had learned in many years in politics—about how to work the system, how to get people to do what I wanted, how to get back at them when they wouldn't. And none of that had worked. There seemed to be no fruitful avenue I could take. The committee was condemned to death. I could not will it into a longer life.

Sensing my frustration and anger, my wife, Janet, said to me one evening, "Tony, have you thought about going on a fast?"

It was a startling question, because I actually had considered fasting a couple of weeks earlier. I had set the thought aside because our twelve-year-old son, Matt, was battling cancer, and I didn't think it would be good for the family if I intentionally put myself through an ordeal. Matt had now finished a round of chemotherapy and was back in school, however. And a fast had enormous appeal.

For one thing, it was a way I could do *something*. More important, fasting has long played a powerful role in faith. A real fast would be an act of self-denial, focusing not on myself but on God. (In my anger, I had been focusing passionately on myself.) I thought it would be especially appropriate to fast because of hunger. Then Janet and I read chapter 58 of Isaiah, and the appropriateness became brilliantly clear:

> *Is not this the fast that I choose [God says through the prophet]:*
>   *to loose the bonds of injustice,*
>   *to undo the thongs of the yoke,*
>   *to let the oppressed go free,*
>   *and to break every yoke?*
> *Is it not to share your bread with the hungry,*
>   *and bring the homeless poor into your house;*
> *when you see the naked, to cover them,*
>   *and not to hide yourself from your own kin? . . .*
> *If you remove the yoke from among you,*
>   *the pointing of the finger, the speaking of evil,*
> *if you offer your food to the hungry*
>   *and satisfy the needs of the afflicted,*
> *then your light shall rise in the darkness*
>   *and your gloom be like the noonday.*
> *The* LORD *will guide you continually,*
>   *and satisfy your needs in parched places,*
>   *and make your bones strong.*
>
>   (verses 6–7, 9–11)

This fast would be a new way for me to bring God into my workplace. While it would be a great spiritual journey for me, a way to ease the pain I was suffering because of the death of my committee, it also would provide a new vehicle for me to reach out to the people (and maybe my colleagues in Congress), to call their attention to hunger, and to ask them to do something about it.

It was not easy for me to decide to take this step, however. I wondered, *How will my colleagues react? My constituents in Dayton, Ohio?* Would they understand that I was fasting, not as a protest, but as a personal act of witness, a way to ask God to help me through this difficult time, and an attempt to show others that hunger is not a problem that we should ignore? Would they understand that it was not a hunger strike—which is a threat to starve oneself, even to death, unless some demand is met? Would I be committing political suicide? Would I be perceived as a flake? Would I become a laughingstock?

A public fast would be completely out of character for Tony Hall the congressman. I had never sought bright spotlights. I had never tried to call attention to myself, other than as it was necessary to win elections and continue to do the work I loved. I had always been a team player, an insider. My other committee assignment was Rules, the ultimate insiders' committee. The Rules Committee had just thirteen members—nine Democrats and four Republicans, when Democrats held the majority. Committee members work under the guidance of their party's leaders to set the rules by which almost every piece of legislation is considered by the full House. It is an enormously powerful committee that gets almost no attention from the mass media but avid attention from every member of the House.

Rules Committee members enjoy enormous influence over the other representatives, because every representative from time to time has to make a case at Rules. As an elected politician, I had been able to devote substantial effort to the issues of hunger, poverty, and oppression because I always took good care of my constituents back home as well. I used my Rules Committee membership as a lever in both of those efforts—to pass legislation that helped my district and to advance the interests of the hungry, the poor, and the oppressed. Would I be able to continue doing that if I alienated my colleagues—especially the leaders—by acting in what they might perceive an outrageous fashion?

As I struggled with what to do, I sought advice from people who regularly counseled me in matters of faith and from others who regularly advised me about Congress and politics—and from a few who did both. I was surprised when all of the people of faith believed the fast was absolutely the right path to take. I was not surprised that my congressional staff cautioned me against it. As far as we knew, no member of Congress had ever done anything like this before. My staff worried—as did I—that a fast would be seen as too radical, the people would not understand, and my political career could be destroyed.

I suffered serious bouts of self-doubt, asking myself, *Who do I think I am, to be calling Congress—and the nation—to task?* But I also believed that we in Congress worried far too much about our own reelections and that we did far too little to really lead. And I was concerned enough and angry enough to take a bold stand.

I prayed long and hard over this decision. I prayed especially that I would not look foolish and embarrass myself. I did not want to be seen as a showboater or a clown. Every morning after I woke up but before I climbed out of bed, I would toss and turn and worry. I wondered if I was crazy. I knew that I was scared. But when I prayed, I felt comfort and peace. I felt God was very close. I knew he would have to be close if I were to do this.

Finally, I plunged forward in a true leap of faith. I cast the worldly advice aside and said, "Here I am, God. Lead me. Guide me. I'm at your mercy." From that point forward, as we planned for announcing the fast, I felt a great deal of excitement, intensity, and energy. I continued to pray and to consult with my brothers and sisters in faith. I planned some details with my staff. I consulted doctors and Dick Gregory, who had fasted many times to promote social justice and had become an expert at it. But the trepidation never left me. I kept wondering if I really was capable of the task I had set before myself.

On March 31, 1993, the day the committee died, I held a press conference on a lawn outside the Capitol, announcing that I would begin to fast on April 5, eating nothing and drinking only water. Reporters wrote that I was angry, which I was. The House, I said, "has lost its conscience. Congress is afflicted with famine. We are hungry for heart—heart for the needy, the powerless, and the forgotten. We have shown that we place our own comfort and political security ahead of the well-being of our most vulnerable people. If we're not going to address this issue—the most basic of rights—what do we stand for in Congress?"

But what I really wanted to focus the public's attention on was what we could do together to continue the fight against hunger without the committee's leadership. I recalled that I had led a forty-hour fast in Dayton in 1985 to raise awareness of hunger and to raise money for relief. It had succeeded far beyond my expectations, attracting more than four thousand participants, raising more than $300,000 (which was split between activities in southwestern Ohio and Africa), and inspiring people to get involved in antihunger programs.

This fast would be different, much more of a spiritual experience. I wasn't seeking to raise money. I was asking God to help me through a difficult time.

But I also was, as I said at the press conference, "issuing a call to summon a broad and creative response from all those who share my concern."

First, I explained, "this is a call to the nation to reflect upon what is going on around us in America and in the world concerning hunger. Second, this is a call to the leadership and to the members of Congress to address this situation. Third, this is a call to the nation and members of Congress to fast with me, to share in the physical suffering of the hungry, and to consider how all of us can be moved to make a difference in our communities and in the world."

I acknowledged that the hunger committee would not be reconstituted, but I requested that Congress create some kind of permanent organization to address the issue. I asked for a national conference on food security. And I said I was looking for some new or increased effort to fight hunger overseas.

To the inevitable question of how long I would fast, I said I didn't know. I explained that I would not injure my health but that I was determined to continue until I was assured in my heart that the awareness of hunger—and America's conscience—had been raised to a higher level.

If people fast and meditate and discover what it's like to go hungry for a while, I thought, *maybe they'll become committed to helping us solve this problem.* But I really didn't have a plan. I didn't have a list of demands to be met. I didn't have a private checklist of responses that would cause me to decide the fast was a success. I just placed myself in God's hands and embarked on an adventure with an unknown destination.

Several of my House colleagues attended the press conference and said they would join me for part of the fast, as did some antihunger activists. Elsewhere in the country, other activists announced that they, too, would fast in solidarity. But I wondered how many others would understand. And the signs were not auspicious the next morning, when I went to a regularly scheduled congressional prayer breakfast and my colleagues avoided talking with me.

On April 4 I had my last pre-fast meal—a great American feast of fried chicken, mashed potatoes, gravy, Caesar salad, shoofly pie, and white wine. On April 6 I boarded a plane for some meetings in Dayton during Congress's Easter/Passover recess. While in flight, I again stewed in anxiety. *My constituents won't understand, and they'll stop supporting me,* I thought. *My colleagues will shun me.*

I also worried about the physical aspects of not eating for an extended time. Dick Gregory had described to me the various stages of hunger and said the desire to eat eventually would subside. He advised that I fill myself with water in the early days as a way of easing the hunger pangs. Doctors in the Capitol Physician's Office didn't want me to do this, and they asked me to let them examine me every week. Other doctors reminded me that the human body is a remarkably resilient machine. A healthy person can fast from one to two months without suffering irreversible harm. The body survives by drawing protein from fat and muscle. Because I was five foot nine and weighed 180 pounds, one doctor noted wryly, I would have "reserves to draw on." Janet also commented that it would do me good to lose some weight. These assurances did not stop me from worrying about how bad I would feel when I became hungry, however. Other than those forty hours in 1985, my only experience with fasting was in connection with a Wednesday morning prayer group. And I always felt famished by eleven o'clock in the morning!

On the other hand, I was so angry with Congress that I wasn't sure I really cared what my colleagues would think or really cared if I might lose my next election. I had now crossed a bridge, I realized, and had blown it up behind me. I felt at peace in God's care. And the next three weeks turned out to be a triumph beyond my wildest imagination.

After my plane touched down in Dayton, I went to Courthouse Square, a plaza in the center of the city, where about three hundred people had gathered to demonstrate solidarity with my fast. Principal Theodore Wallace of Chaminade-Julienne, a Roman Catholic high school in Dayton, announced that he would fast with me for three days that week. About 340 C-J students, along with 60 parents and staff, pledged to forgo at least one meal and to donate the value of the meal to the Dayton Area Emergency Food Bank. Noting that this was the week before Easter, Mr. Wallace said fasting would be particularly timely as we would reflect on Christ's suffering on Good Friday. About forty students at the University of Dayton, another Roman Catholic school, also joined the fast. A CBS News crew traveled with me from Washington and spent three days in Dayton preparing a report. I was thrilled at the support and the attention from the media, but I also felt terribly hungry, and I was losing energy very quickly.

The media presented a truly pleasant surprise. I had no idea how they'd react, and it turned out they reacted quite positively. Numerous reporters became interested in the story, and they covered it fairly, accurately (for the most part), and frequently. I also received favorable commentary from editorial writers and columnists on the right as well as the left. My hometown newspaper, the *Dayton Daily News*, covered the fast thoroughly and supported me repeatedly in editorials and columns. My sincerity must have appeared evident, because I received compliments even from commentators who approved the death of the select committees. *Roll Call*, Capitol Hill's local newspaper, for instance, called the select committees "redundant" and said they "had to go." But in the same editorial, the paper said, "At a time when politicians are so calculating and 'responsive' that they often can't remember what they really believe, it's refreshing to see a congressman who cares so much about a cause. We admire Hall for his courage and for setting an offbeat but inspirational example to colleagues who, from time to time, need to be shaken up."[1]

Physically and psychologically, the first week of the fast was the hardest. I was horribly hungry—I could say "in agony"—and getting weaker by the day. I thought constantly about what I would like to eat—that last meal of fried chicken, mashed potatoes, and Caesar salad; some future meals with some of my favorite foods, such as steak, roast beef, and key lime pie. But I also thought about all the people who have no realistic hope for a future meal of any kind, and I found the strength to continue.

Family mealtimes were the worst. I couldn't go to the table because the food would be too tempting, and not being able to eat it would be agonizing. Janet, Matt, and Jyl would try to hide from me when they snacked between meals. So I spent these times alone, praying, reading, thinking about what I was doing, and contemplating the importance of the family meal. Normally, we probably don't think about how much mealtime means to the family. But it's one of the few times when we all sit down together and talk about the day, the week—about anything.

I followed Dick Gregory's advice to fill up on water. I really poured it down. Since it was the only thing I was consuming, I paid a great deal more attention to it than I ever had before. I really noticed the difference in taste when I drank from the tap at home, the office, or someplace else. My sense of smell also heightened throughout the fast. I could tell what people had eaten because their bodies gave off aromas that I had never noticed before.

The hardest day of the fast came on Easter, which was my seventh day without eating. Janet and I had gone on a retreat in Maryland with some friends, and our friends prepared a typical big American holiday dinner—turkey, potatoes, dressing, pie, cake. It drove me nuts. I had to leave them, go outside and take a walk, to get away from those wonderful aromas. I decided that if I could get through this day, I would be over the hump. I did, and I was.

Just as Dick Gregory said, the sensation of hunger faded in about a week. It's as if the body gives up on getting food and stops demanding it. From then on, I could join my family at mealtimes and not be bothered a bit. It was a revelation about the poor and the hungry, to whom I came to feel exceptionally close as the fast went on. I now fully understood, in a way I never had before, a strange phenomenon I had witnessed during famines: starving children who refused to eat when food was finally offered to them.

The absence of hunger pangs did not mean I wasn't feeling the physical effects of the fast, however. I'd wake up in the morning feeling fine. My head would be clear. I would think I had lots of energy. But after noon, I would fade. The energy would desert me and weakness would take over. I'd need to nap. Then, when I woke from the nap, I'd feel like I couldn't get up because I was so tired. Lacking the fuel of food, my body temperature apparently dropped, and I felt cold all the time. It also seemed my brain slowed down in the afternoon; I felt "dull." I thought of poor children who don't do well in school, who fall asleep in the afternoon, who become poor students because of poor nutrition. Remarkably, some of my vital signs—blood pressure, the results of blood tests—actually improved.

Oddly, I also sometimes felt lonely, even though I knew I was getting a great deal of support. Part of that feeling stemmed from my inability to shake my worries about what people really thought of what I was doing.

Because of the recess, I couldn't judge the reaction of Congress during the first two weeks of the fast. Throughout the country, however, the outpouring of support was overwhelming. I appeared on numerous television and radio programs, and the fast was written about in newspapers everywhere. Humanitarian organizations put the word out to their supporters.

Groups organized supportive events. Individuals from every state wrote me incredibly moving letters.

The people of Dayton were particularly supportive, organizing rallies, prayer vigils, and even a parade! Thousands of people wrote messages on paper plates—protesting the death of the hunger committee and calling for a replacement—and mailed them to Congress. More than fifteen thousand high school and college students from thirty-four states participated in antihunger activities organized by the National Student Campaign against Hunger and Homelessness. Students in two thousand high schools and two hundred colleges joined the fast. Religious groups took actions in support. Seventeen presidents and CEOs of major humanitarian organizations bought a full-page ad in *Roll Call* to publicly request that President Clinton hold a national summit on hunger. Actors Jeff Bridges and Valerie Harper organized a celebrity fast to call attention to the issue. Among the eclectic group of celebrities who stopped eating for a day were Susan Sarandon, Graham Nash, Phyllis Diller, the late Steve Allen, Edward James Olmos, Cassandra "Elvira" Peterson, former astronaut Buzz Aldrin, and basketball star Olden Polynice.

The House got back to business after the recess on April 19, and it quickly became clear that the representatives hadn't missed the public response to my call for action against hunger. They had read about it in their hometown newspapers, perhaps seen a report on a network television program. In many of their districts, schools, religious institutions, or local chapters of humanitarian organizations had taken action. For the members of Congress, this really was bringing it all back home—the place most of them look for their directions. A *Washington Post* writer observed "at least a puzzled acknowledgment from his Hill colleagues that something unusual is going on here."[2]

On April 20, I went to the House floor for the first time since beginning the fast and attended my first Rules Committee meeting. I was so weak, I had to ask an aide to drive me from my office building to the Capitol because I could walk only short distances without becoming exhausted. The other representatives treated me quite a bit differently from the way they had three weeks before. They wanted to talk with me. They were warm. They commented on my loss of weight. They inquired about my health. They were curious about what was happening to my body.

As that third week of my fast rolled on, people from around the country continued to rally at my side. As the days added up to weeks, people realized how committed I really was to this cause, and their support grew deeper. Now, with Washington full of government officials once again, the big and powerful institutions began to respond—with the "leaders" following the people, as they almost always do.

I knew the time to end the fast was nearing when I received a phone call from my friend Bill Stanton, a former Republican representative from Ohio who now was an executive at the World Bank, the planet's richest financier of development in the third world. "Tony," he said, "we're really moved by your fast, and we are prepared to have a world conference on hunger and put money behind it." Because of the fast, he said, colleagues at the bank had approached him, asking if he knew me and if he understood what I was up to. Their inquiry, Bill explained, led to discussions about what the bank could do to elevate awareness of hunger and how it might be able to direct more of its resources to attacking the problem.

When the conference was held in Washington that November, participants included former U.S. president Jimmy Carter, who has devoted his postpresidential life to promoting peace and bettering the lot of the poor; United Nations secretary general Boutros Boutros-Ghali; World Bank president Lewis Preston; President Ketumile Masire of Botswana; the World Bank's senior managers; and representatives of many humanitarian organizations that do the real work of bringing relief and education directly to the poor and hungry. The bank announced that as a symbolic gesture designed to inspire others to take similar action, it would make a $2 million grant to the Grameen Trust, an affiliate of the Grameen Bank, one of the most effective antipoverty organizations in the world, which makes small loans to help poor people start small businesses. World Bank officials also said they would ask the bank's sponsoring governments for permission to expand its direct work with the poor.

Muhammad Yunus, Grameen's founder, later told me that my fast, the conference, and the World Bank's actions gave a significant boost to Grameen specifically and to microenterprise in general. The fast and the conference drew attention to hunger and poverty, he said. Many more people and institutions became aware of the value of Grameen and microfinance. Financial support for the microenterprise movement jumped around the world. Since the fast, the World Bank alone has increased its microfinance portfolio to more than $1 billion.

Other signs that the fast had raised awareness included a letter from President Clinton—who, with Vice President Gore, had joined the fast briefly—acknowledging my "moral leadership on this vital issue." A special House-Senate committee on congressional reform invited me to testify about my call for a permanent committee to focus on human needs. The House Democratic Caucus—which includes all Democratic representatives—invited me to speak about what they could do to respond to the hunger committee's death. And the Agriculture Department announced that—complementing the World Bank's plans—it would conduct a national conference on domestic hunger and a series of regional conferences. The national conference was held in Washington in June and was followed by regional gatherings in Vermont, Texas, Missouri, and, finally, Dayton.

With the Agriculture Department announcement on Monday, April 26, 1993—made by Secretary Mike Espy, a former Mississippi congressman who had chaired the hunger committee's Domestic Task Force—I concluded it was time to end the fast. Because the fast had been a very public endeavor, I thought the breaking of it should be as well. I invited some reporters to my office, and in keeping with an advertising slogan at the time, I had a V-8.

I hadn't eaten for twenty-two days, and that thick, salty vegetable juice tasted exceptionally good. I thought I could pick out the taste of each of the vegetables that had been liquefied and mixed into this marvelous elixir— tomatoes, beets, celery, carrots, lettuce, spinach, parsley, and watercress. Well, maybe not the parsley and watercress. Unfortunately, I could only sip a little bit. Because my stomach had essentially been shut down for three weeks, I would have to coax it gradually back to use, maybe not being able to enjoy a full meal until the end of the week. I had lost twenty-three pounds—dropping from a robust 180 to a gaunt 157—and I joked that I would enjoy putting every single pound back on. A reporter asked what I would have for that first full meal, and I joked again, rattling off a long list: "Fried chicken, maybe a nice steak, maybe some blackberry pie, mashed potatoes and gravy, shoofly pie, some pasta, ice cream . . .

"The wonderful thing," I added, "is I knew I could end my fast, and I was going to end it, and I had hope of someday looking forward to good food. There are so many people in the world who don't have that hope—who don't have any idea where the next meal is going to come from—and that was what the fast was all about."

The following few days were a whirlwind of activity, and I overdid it a bit—especially the return to eating. I was told to go slow, starting with small amounts of juice, fruit, and yogurt, and to stay away from meat for at least seven days. After three days, I felt so good that I ate veal and spaghetti with meat sauce. The reward for this boldness consisted of severe stomach cramps and the realization that I should pay attention to people who know what they're talking about.

The most emotional moment of the week came at the Democratic caucus on Wednesday, in the ornate, historic House Chamber, closed to all but Democratic representatives. When I walked in, these legislators—who had let my committee die and who had been put off by my decision to fast—gave me a standing ovation. Now, not only did they approve of what I had done, but they were excited about it. I chuckled to myself as I noted this adjustment in attitude, but I admonished myself to keep this change in perspective. My emotions were mixed. I was honored, but I also realized just how fickle the political system can be.

I talked to the caucus for half an hour, from notes and from my heart. I reviewed the history of the committee—why it was created in 1984 (because the issue was not being adequately addressed); how Mickey Leland, the first committee chairman, was killed in a plane crash in Ethiopia while on a committee mission in 1989; why I fasted; and why I believed the committee's work wasn't finished.

"There are many great individuals in this body, full of character and dignity and integrity," I said as I concluded my remarks. "But as a body, we lack intensity for issues like these. We used to have it. We used to speak and advocate for the hungry. We used to be a force to be reckoned with. Now it seems we spend all our time worrying about the rich. Somewhere along the line, we lost our voice for the voiceless, the have-nots, the children, the widows, the orphans, the people who stink and don't look so good.

"Let's get it back. We still have time."

When I stopped talking, they gave me another standing ovation. After the meeting, they made me feel even better by what they said to reporters when I wasn't around.

Dick Gephardt, the majority leader, said I had delivered one of the most memorable speeches he had heard during sixteen years in Congress. "He made us feel uncomfortable," Dick said, "because we hadn't better understood what he was trying to do and the depth of his feeling about it."[3] Steny Hoyer, the caucus chair, said there was now "very broad support" for focusing on the issue. "Congressman Hall has done a great service to the country," he said.[4] Ted Strickland, a newly elected representative from Ohio and a committee supporter, said that "a lot of the members felt chagrined."[5] Many freshman legislators didn't understand the importance of the committee until the fast caught their attention, Ted explained. The next day, I attended the same prayer breakfast gathering at which my colleagues had avoided me at the outset of the fast. This time they, too, stood and applauded.

More important, these lawmakers promised to follow through on the issue. And they did. The bipartisan Congressional Hunger Caucus was created to carry on the hunger committee's work. A caucus, unfortunately, is not entitled to the same resources as a committee; caucus members fund the caucus's work with contributions from their personal office budgets (mostly mine), for instance. But we did have an office, a small staff, and a vehicle for investigating and publicizing the problems of hunger and for advocating solutions. Also with bipartisan cooperation, we created the Congressional Hunger Center, which is led by members of the House and Senate who care about the issue but is an independent organization that does not rely on congressional fickleness for its survival. The center encourages antihunger activities, provides a forum for sharing hunger information, and trains young people for careers in organizations that are working to end hunger.

A year later I fasted again—for three days during Holy Week—to remember that hunger still remained an enormous problem and that we could solve it. "A desperate situation requires something out of the ordinary," I said in talking publicly about this 1994 fast and inviting others to join me. "With a fast, you deny yourself something in order to focus on something bigger." This time President Clinton, Vice President Gore, and more than a score of my congressional colleagues participated in at least part of my fast.

To me, the value of the fast extended far beyond those specific accomplishments, because I learned—or perhaps I should say relearned—two important lessons.

The first is that if you let him, God will use you. No matter how small the work or how large the work, if you want to be used, you will be. That's how God works. He works through people. When I looked back on the fast, I realized that the things I planned didn't turn out nearly as well as the things I didn't plan. And actually, I didn't plan very much. There was no way I could imagine in advance the public reaction to what I did. And the most important thing I did was to announce the fast and ask God to guide me through it. Then good things happened. And they weren't all in the realm of public action.

As I was trying to decide whether to begin the fast, I knew I would need God to be near me. I asked him to be, and I discovered throughout the fast that he was. He fed me, not with food, but with his purpose. It was as Jesus said in Matthew 4:4: "One does not live by bread alone, but by every word that comes from the mouth of God." It didn't matter how the rest of the world reacted to my efforts, because God does not call us to be successful. He calls us to be faithful. And I was trying to be faithful to his clear admonition that we help those in need. Janet said to me afterward that she saw a spirit on me during the fast that she had never seen before and hadn't seen since. I was at peace and filled with joy, and it showed.

I also found myself feeling much closer to the hungry, poor, and oppressed people I had been trying to help for so long. Because I knew my fast would end, not to mention that it would end at the time of my choosing, I could not really have the same experience as those starving people who may never have another meal. But I did learn what it feels like to be without food for a substantial time, and God did make me feel closer to those whom Jesus called "the least of these" as he informed us of our duty to help them.

I noticed that some of these blessings extended to my family. Because of Matt's illness, we had experienced a lot of stress. During the fast, the stress was lifted. We all were comforted and had peace. Janet, Jyl, and Matt were totally supportive. Jyl fasted a bit herself. One of the great untold stories about this experience is that my minister, Jim Hutchens, fasted with me for the full three weeks.

The second lesson is that if you show the American people a need, and a way to address that need, they will respond. Americans aren't indifferent to the needs of the poor; they're just too often unaware. And their "leaders" in government are too often afraid to challenge the people to act.

People are crying out for leaders. They want their leaders to be out in front of them, not looking back or unsure of which direction to go. They want to be guided. They want to see examples.

If you touch Americans—touch their hearts—they become emotional, they become excited, they become passionate. If you educate them and then lead them, they will help. And they will figure out how to further the cause in even better ways.

CHAPTER 7

BRINGING IT ALL BACK HOME

*Doing What's
in Front of Dayton*

＊ ＊ ＊

After I returned from Ethiopia and began devoting more time to the global hunger problem, I started hearing disturbing comments from some of my constituents. Even before I went to Ethiopia, I had begun learning about human rights abuses around the world because of my membership in the Foreign Relations Committee, and I had started to take some action against them. I criticized U.S. support for Ferdinand Marcos's repressive regime in the Philippines, for instance, and I protested Indonesia's occupation of the tiny independent nation of East Timor.

Not many Daytonians were aware of the appalling policies of Marcos, who justified his assaults on Filipinos' freedoms on the grounds that he was fighting a Communist insurgency. Needless to say, almost no one in Dayton had even heard of East Timor. When news media reports about my efforts on behalf of Ethiopia were added to earlier reports about my involvement with the Philippines, East Timor, and other far-off places, I started receiving letters that advanced this common theme: You care more about people on the other side of the world than you care about us; so what good are you to Dayton?

People were stopping me on the street to deliver the same message. Even my friends, trying to seem understanding and supportive, were saying things such as, "You know, Tony, we appreciate your work in the Philippines, and it's really special, and you seem to be the only guy who really cares about it. But we've got problems here in Dayton, too, and you need to do something about them."

With even friends and supporters raising these concerns, I knew I was in trouble. If I wanted to use Congress's bully pulpit to promote humanitarian causes, I would have to be reelected. But I wouldn't win many more elections if Dayton voters didn't see a connection between my work and my district. I had to convince my constituents that my humanitarian work was worthwhile. I had to bring the issue home—not just by revealing the hunger and poverty that existed in my Third Congressional District but also by involving the people of Dayton in my work.

I gathered my staff together and told them, "You and I know I care about my district, but the perception is I care more about what happens outside the district than about what happens here. We've got to bring this issue home— we've got to educate our constituents about this issue—or I won't be able to do this anymore, because they're going to vote me out."

We brainstormed and came up with an idea that was based on the popular fund-raising scheme in which people walk or run or ride bikes or do any number of other activities to attract donations to some charitable cause. What better way to raise money and call attention to hunger, we thought, than with a fast? It would be symbolic. And participants would gain some understanding of what hungry people go through when they can't find enough to eat. We asked people to stop eating for forty hours, from Friday evening until Sunday afternoon, and to solicit pledges from friends and relatives based on the amount of time they fasted. My good friend Nick Sabatino came up with a slogan—"Stop Hunger Fast"—with more than one meaning. It connoted ending hunger quickly, but it also implied that you could help end hunger by fasting.

This was in May 1985, long before the twenty-two-day fast I undertook when Congress abolished the Select Committee on Hunger in 1993. It was of far shorter duration. And it was conceived in much different circumstances. But it had the same purpose of making people think about—and, we hoped, begin to act on—this often-overlooked problem. Like my lengthy fast, it also turned out to be far more successful than I could have imagined.

We wanted to draw connections between Dayton and hungry people in other countries, both by teaching Daytonians that there is hunger in our community and by getting them involved in fighting hunger at home and abroad. Five African diplomats—including the ambassadors of Sierra Leone and

Uganda—came to Dayton to talk about the needs in their countries. Sinclair Community College gave us space on its downtown Dayton campus, where we set up exhibits and sold African wares, as well as items to commemorate the fast, such as T-shirts, posters, and buttons. Africans who were living in the Dayton area taught about life and culture in their homelands. Events also were held at Wright State University, just outside the city. The whole thing turned into a kind of festival.

Janet joined me in the fast, and we brought Jyl and Matt along to witness the events. People in high schools, colleges, churches, and synagogues got together to participate. Young people got their parents to make pledges. I recruited some businesses to join my friends in making contributions.

By the time we broke the fast with Sunday brunch at Sinclair, some four thousand people had participated, raising more than $300,000 in the process. We donated half to relief activities in Africa and half to organizations that helped the hungry in southwestern Ohio.

More important, four thousand people of many ages, religions, and political persuasions had taken action against hunger, learned something about its presence in Dayton as well as overseas, felt a little bit of what it's like to be hungry, and begun to understand why I had become devoted to working on this issue. We had started to build a constituency for fighting hunger among the people of my congressional district. Daytonians over time not only would come to accept the idea of their congressman devoting a portion of his efforts to the hungry but would become involved themselves in creative and effective ways. They volunteered to work with existing organizations, and they created new projects of their own.

The previous winter, I had helped to organize a hot-lunch program for senior citizens on weekends. The federal government funded a meals-for-seniors program, but it provided meals only Monday through Friday. Particularly in the winter, when older folks have more difficulty getting around, not having weekend meals created a hardship.

We sought support for resuming the program in the winter of 1985, and the community's response was wonderful. The Ponderosa Steakhouse chain, then headquartered in Dayton, had acquired a prizewinning steer. The company had the steer butchered and donated the meat to the program. Local restaurants pledged either food or money. The Miami Valley Restaurant Association made a financial contribution. Other businesses recruited volunteers. The program became so popular that more people volunteered than we could put to work.

Dayton residents also leaped at the opportunity to collect unharvested fruits and vegetables from farmers' fields and donate them to food programs. A lot of people told me the plan was ingenious, but I had to confess that I didn't think it up. Gleaning appears in the earliest books of the Bible, where God instructs farmers to leave some of their crops for the poor (see Leviticus 19:10; Deuteronomy 24:21).

Americans waste food in unbelievable quantities. Some of the waste occurs simply because harvesting is inherently inefficient. Mechanical harvesters always leave food behind. Even hand pickers fail to harvest everything. They have to move pretty quickly, and some pieces are just too hard to get. We Americans also are quite fussy about our food. It not only has to be safe and tasty; it has to look good. Perfectly healthy food is discarded simply because of its appearance.

Since food is so plentiful here, we don't worry about waste. Restaurants cook more than they will sell and throw away the leftovers at the end of the day. In almost every family, a regular chore is searching through the refrigerator to find food that has gone bad and must be pitched. I've been told that more than one hundred million tons of food go to waste in our country every year. I saw the truth of all this firsthand when one Dayton-area farmer took me to a cornfield after I asked if we could glean on his land.

"You might as well take this entire field," the farmer said, gesturing at the growing corn, which looked perfectly fine to my untrained eyes.

"Can't you sell it?" I asked.

"It's kind of imperfect," he replied, showing me some ears with missing kernels. "Americans are particular. Most Americans shopping in a grocery store aren't going to buy this corn. If you don't take it, the crows will get it, or we'll just plow it under."

Another farmer showed me a field of strawberries that farmworkers already had harvested by hand. Many berries were left for our gleaners to collect.

The Stop Hunger Fast had produced a roster of people and organizations who wanted to help, so it was easy for us to recruit gleaners. The only tricky part was pulling enough volunteers together on short notice. Sometimes a farmer would inform us that a field had just been harvested and we needed to glean right away.

Just as the fast turned into a festival, the days of gleaning became times of great fun. Adults, kids, people of many religions, middle-class people, rich people, and some of the poor themselves joined the gleaning crews. And they came back when we needed them again.

That first year, 1986, nine farmers let us into their fields, where our gleaners salvaged more than twenty tons of fresh produce that went to feed the poor. Just as I have said so often about my humanitarian projects, this gleaning project "surpassed all our expectations," in the words of Kipra Holley, who ran our local Red Cross Emergency Resource Bank's food center. Kipra made that comment to an Associated Press reporter whose story about gleaning helped me to understand the need for leadership and the fact that Americans will respond when leaders call them to do good things.

The story reported that an attempt to glean in the Cincinnati area had not gone well. The director of a local service organization said the problem was that no public official had gotten out front to urge people to get involved, the way I had. All I had to do was get the ball rolling, and the people of Dayton created a success. The next year, I started promoting gleaning around Ohio, and over the following years, hundreds of tons of food were salvaged in our state.

Gleaning has been around a lot longer than I have, and people were gleaning elsewhere in America before we started our program in Dayton. But we did a particularly effective job of it. I used my bully pulpit to promote it around the country. People came to study our program. So we had an effect beyond simply feeding hungry people in our own community.

As we carried out projects and received publicity for them, we inspired more people to get involved. As Daytonians learned about our antihunger efforts and saw that they worked, our volunteers begat more volunteers. Some of them invented new projects that I never would have dreamed of.

We were building a constituency for the hungry. Daytonians were, as Mother Teresa had advised, doing what was in front of them. As the point man on the issue, I received many calls from people who wanted to help. Not surprisingly, a lot of the calls came from people in the food business. Owners and managers of hotels, restaurants, catering services, country clubs, hospitals—anyplace that served meals—phoned with the same message: "We always prepare more food than we serve," they said. "We always end up just throwing it away. We hate the waste, but we don't know what to do about it."

In 1989, working with the Emergency Resource Bank, I arranged for a refrigerated truck to collect surplus food from these establishments and deliver it to food pantries and soup kitchens. Unfortunately, after this project had been in operation for a while, I came to realize that it cost about as much to rent the truck and pay the driver as it would to simply buy an equivalent amount of food in the first place. While giving otherwise-wasted food to the hungry seemed to be a great idea, our project didn't make practical sense.

I discussed my frustration with this dilemma one day while participating in a talk show on Dayton's WHIO radio station. Among the listeners was Bruce Feldman, president of Economy Linen and Towel Service, who had tuned in to WHIO while driving home from work. Since 1931 his family's company has supplied institutions in the Dayton area and elsewhere with uniforms, tablecloths, napkins, towels, and other such products. His clients were the institutions that wanted to donate their surplus food to the poor. He phoned me with an idea. Every day, his trucks visited his clients, delivered clean linens, and picked up soiled linens to be laundered. Why couldn't they pick up food too?

It took a lot of planning on Bruce's part, but he was able to launch Operation Food Share in May 1990. Economy Linen trucks started picking up food from seventeen institutions with food-service operations—seven restaurants, two caterers, four country clubs, three private clubs, and the University of Dayton. Other companies and civic organizations donated equipment or money.

The food service organizations froze their leftovers and placed them in insulated containers. During their regular rounds, Economy Linen drivers picked up those containers and dropped off empty sanitized containers for use the next day. The drivers took the food to Economy Linen's plant, where it was stored in a freezer. It then was transferred to the Emergency Resource Bank. Soup kitchens, food pantries, and homeless shelters in three counties could draw on this new source of food.

In the first year, Economy Linen's trucks salvaged more than twenty-five thousand pounds of food that otherwise would have been thrown away. They collected another fifteen thousand pounds in the next six months. By the mid-1990s, they were providing more than one hundred thousand pounds of good food each year to the poor.

But Bruce didn't stop there. Working through the Textile Rental Services Association of America, his industry's trade organization, Bruce urged other companies to adopt Operation Food Share in their communities. The first started operating in Washington in 1992, and companies in other cities followed suit.

I never would have known how to create Operation Food Share on my own. But as I have found repeatedly, if you bring a need to the attention of the American people, they will respond. And by responding, as Bruce Feldman showed, one person can make a huge difference. Later I got to thinking that my political party could make a difference, too, beyond simply electing people to office.

The Montgomery County Democratic Party owns a two-story building in downtown Dayton, most of which was going unused most of the time. Our small staff works in its offices daily, but the offices occupy just a fraction of the building. The rest of the space—a large meeting room on the first floor and smaller rooms on the second—was being underutilized.

About a block away, the Society of St. Vincent de Paul operated a homeless shelter, which they named the St. Vincent Hotel. Unfortunately, demand for beds—especially in cold weather—far exceeded the facility's capacity. *Why don't we open a shelter in our building to pick up the emergency overflow?* I thought to myself.

Dennis Lieberman, the party chairman, embraced the idea. Support wasn't unanimous, however. Some people simply believed that a political party really does have just one function—winning elections. Moving beyond that, they argued, would be inappropriate. Others, like many Americans, feared getting too close to the homeless. The headquarters served as a bit of a social center for some people who would come in, play cards, and chat with friends. They worried that the people who needed shelter would damage the property and leave the place dirty.

I argued back that it was more than appropriate for us to open an overflow shelter in our building—that we should consider it an obligation. "We like to call ourselves the party of the people," I said, "the party that represents the middle class, the workers, and the poor. If that's true, we should feel ashamed if all we do is talk about it. This building is a great asset. How can we justify not using it to help the people we claim to represent? If we really care for the poor, let's prove it by extending our hands to the homeless people who are, literally, right outside our front door."

With the party chairman and the congressman leading the way, that argument carried the day. We put beds, clean linens, and a little bit of food in two rooms upstairs, and we started taking in women and children when the St. Vincent shelter overflowed. It was a clean, warm, comfortable, and safe place for them to stay, and it became an essential part of St. Vincent's mission. The success of the shelter inspired us to open a food pantry at our headquarters. Then we opened our big first-floor meeting room to serve hot meals to the poor and homeless on Saturday afternoons.

When Dennis and I held a press conference to unveil our shelter during the winter of 1995, we were able to demonstrate that our Democratic Party really does care for the poor. We put our money—our assets—where our mouths were. And we became one more example of the good works that built the constituency for the hungry and the poor in my hometown.

By the mid-1990s, it seemed that everyone in the Dayton area had joined that constituency. When help was needed, a call went out and someone responded. And it didn't have to be a need in Dayton. Once, for instance, while I was investigating hunger and poverty in Appalachian Ohio, I asked Rev. Mel Franklin what one thing he would wish for to improve life in his little town of McArthur.

Rev. Franklin, whose United Methodist church ran a food pantry, replied, "Transportation from where we are in southeastern Ohio to where the jobs are. We don't have many jobs here. The unemployment rate is high. We've got a video store here that advertised a job for a clerk, and 250 people applied. If we had transportation, we could take people to where the jobs are around Columbus in the morning and bring them back home at night."

When I went back to Dayton, I told this minister's story to leaders of several unions that had many members with relatives in Appalachia. The Miami Valley Regional Transit Authority donated a retired bus.

Volunteer mechanics put new tires on the bus and fixed up the engine. Working with a group called Our Common Heritage—an organization of Dayton-area residents with Appalachian roots—the union members raised money for the project. Then a bunch of the people who had been involved hopped on that bus and took it to McArthur—along with a $2,500 donation to Rev. Franklin's food pantry. When we pulled into town, we discovered that the people there had posted signs along the road to welcome and thank us.

Because of these Daytonians' Appalachian heritage, they were especially proud and excited about what they'd done, and the project was exceptionally meaningful to them. That trip from the flatland of Dayton to the hills of Appalachia was festive and full of joy—more fun, I think, for the people who were giving than for the people who received.

Rev. Franklin took that bus and did exactly what he said he'd do—drove workers to newfound jobs in the Columbus area in the morning and returned them home at night.

All of these projects produced the twin benefits of helping the poor and the hungry and teaching the people of Dayton about problems and ways that individuals can help. In addition, they also served as models for other communities to emulate, and they educated me about how to make good things happen.

Helping those in need takes leadership and commitment. But it doesn't require a large number of leaders or a heroic investment of time and effort. And *anyone* can take the lead. All you need are two or three people who acquire a vision, catch fire to fulfill it, and remain dedicated to the task. People will follow if they sense you're sincere and want to do good. When you lead by example, others will take up the cause, and some of them will become leaders too.

All of these projects demonstrated what private individuals and organizations can accomplish with little or no government assistance and a relatively small amount of money. Individual programs don't necessarily last forever. Some die, and others are born. What's important is that many people in Dayton are committed to helping the less fortunate. They've learned that doing good can be both personally fulfilling and a great deal of fun.

As a congressman who had to run for reelection every other year, I commissioned a lot of public opinion surveys. Early in my congressional career, poverty and foreign affairs were at the bottom of the issues Daytonians said they cared about. Over the years, those issues rose to second and third in my polls.

In my later years in Congress, we also asked people what they would want to talk about if they had a chance to talk with me. Almost 80 percent said they'd like to talk about hunger.

Right up through my last campaign, I faced opponents who charged that I cared more about Africa than I cared about Dayton, that I cared too much about the poor and not enough about the middle class, that I didn't take care of my district's parochial interests. After I won my first few reelections, I stopped worrying about those attacks. People would ask me how I was going to answer the attacks, and I'd say, "I'm not going to answer them. I don't have to answer them." I *did* look after my district's parochial interests, and my constituents knew that. More significant, my polls showed that the vast majority of Daytonians loved my work on hunger, poverty, and human rights. They believed it was important. Best of all, they embraced it as their own.

CHAPTER 8

THE UNITED STATES

*Finding and Fighting
Hunger and Poverty
Around the Corner and
Over the Hill*

* * *

Many of my constituents, including a lot of my Dayton friends, have roots sunk deep into Appalachia. They—or their parents or grandparents—left the rural hills and hollows of southeastern Ohio, Kentucky, West Virginia, and other parts of that region to take good-paying jobs in Dayton's factories when America's heavy industries were booming. Unlike those who complained I wasn't paying enough attention to my district's parochial concerns, these constituents urged me to expand my horizons to this poor, rural section of our country they so loved.

"We know there are poor and hungry people down there," these constituents told me. "But we don't know exactly how big the problem is or what might be done about it. Is there a way we can find out what's going on in Appalachia and help the people there?"

Thrilled to have constituents who wanted to do more about hunger, I began to look into the situation. I took trips through southeastern Ohio and nearby states, both to learn and to shine a light on what I discovered. What I found bore no resemblance to the horrors I'd encountered in Ethiopia and other third world trouble spots. But I did meet desperate people and saw sad scenes that have stuck in my memory and fortified my commitment to work for poor and hungry Americans as well as people overseas.

In southeastern Ohio, for instance, I met Darryl and Martha Wagner, an elderly couple who cried as they told me that it was impossible for them to pay all their bills. Once, Martha said, she repeatedly added water to a large can of tomato juice, continually thinning it over a two-week period during which it was their only source of food. She also described preparing an economical "chicken" soup. With an egg and flour, she made noodles for the soup. Then she told Darryl to "just pretend there's chicken in there."

Another elderly couple told me a similar story about a can of soup they watered down at each meal for three days. It was near the end of the month, and they couldn't make their Social Security benefits stretch the full four weeks.

It's a story about hungry children that remains most vivid in my memory, however, and that I return to often when I contemplate our obligation to help the needy. During a trip through southeastern Ohio, I met a single mother who lived with two children in a trailer off a country road. She and the children were among more than three hundred people, old and young, who were standing in line to get free groceries at a food bank that I was visiting in a small town not far from her home. I asked about her needs, and she described how difficult it was to keep her children well fed and how much she depended on the food bank. She did not relate what I later found to be the most compelling part of her story. I would hear that only from a food bank volunteer.

Sometimes, the volunteer told me, he would deliver groceries to this woman's trailer because it was hard for her to get into town. If the children were home when he delivered the food, the volunteer said, they would jump up and down with great excitement and joy. Good food was so scarce in this household that the children celebrated when it arrived.

Whenever I recall that story, I think, *Children should get excited about toys, about candy, about games, about holidays. Children should not get excited about food.* But if food for your family is scarce—if food from the food bank tastes better than the food your mother stretches most other times—then a visit from the food bank volunteer can be reason for joy.

That's the face of hunger and poverty in America today. It's not starvation. It's not cowering in refugee camps. It's these kids getting excited about food. It's old people diluting soup between Social Security checks. It's even families who have long enjoyed the middle-class lifestyle who suddenly fall on hard times and turn to a food bank for assistance. And I worry the problem may get worse as companies abandon pension and health insurance programs for their workers and retirees.

American hunger often hits elderly couples who have worked hard all their lives, have never even thought about needing welfare benefits, and who depend primarily or entirely on Social Security for their income. One of them gets sick, and they discover their health insurance doesn't cover prescription drugs—or they don't have health insurance at all. Their utility bills rise faster than their income. Something breaks at home and requires a costly repair. And they find themselves visiting a food bank or a soup kitchen near the end of every month.

Many of the working poor find themselves in similar situations because their low-paying jobs carry no fringe benefits. If someone gets sick or the car breaks down, there isn't enough money to pay all the bills. They stretch their food, aren't able to buy enough healthful food, and head for the soup kitchen or food bank once a month or so.

Despite the common tendency to equate poverty with urban ghettos, Americans go hungry in the city and the countryside alike, as my trips through Appalachia demonstrated, and as Mike Espy showed me in the South.

When he was chairman of the House hunger committee's Domestic Task Force, Mike asked me to go with him to some of the poorest rural areas in one of the poorest and most rural states in the country, his native Mississippi. Most of the homes we visited there were rickety wooden houses sitting on cinder blocks with no basements. A woodstove was the standard means of heating and cooking. Few of the houses had running water or indoor bathrooms. Some didn't even have outhouses; the family just used a hole dug into the ground out in the woods. Several houses had just one room, which was sparsely furnished; a few houses had only one bed, so the children slept on the floor. In some houses, cloth was tied across the window openings in lieu of glass.

The people living in these houses owned maybe one change of clothes. The clothes they were wearing were tattered and in some cases dirty. The children for the most part didn't wear shoes. The area supported few jobs, so the adults barely scratched out a living, much of it through subsistence farming. They couldn't grow enough, however, so they were hungry.

According to Bread for the World, a respected Christian organization that has been advocating for the hungry for more than thirty years, a larger proportion of Americans go hungry in rural places than in metropolitan areas. Not surprisingly, rural hunger is most prevalent among the poorest rural residents—white Appalachians, blacks in the Deep South, Hispanics in the U.S.-Mexico border region, and Plains Indians. But hunger can be found throughout our rich country.

Some 9.6 million Americans, including 3 million children, live in homes that experience hunger, according to Bread for the World's 2005 report on domestic hunger.[1] That means at least one person in the home frequently skips meals or eats too little at a meal. Sometimes the children go hungry. Many times parents skimp on eating so their children can eat more. Bread for the World says another 26.7 million Americans live in homes that are at risk of hunger. That means they eat a low-quality diet or have to go to food banks or soup kitchens to keep from going hungry.

Although we made great strides against hunger in America throughout the twentieth century, we've been backsliding in the last few years, information collected by Bread for the World shows. The number of Americans in those hungry or at-risk families increased by 1.4 million from 2002 to 2003, the Agriculture Department reported.[2] A U.S. Conference of Mayors survey found that requests for emergency food assistance increased an average of 13 percent from 2003 to 2004.[3] America's Second Harvest, the national food bank network, said the number of people seeking food from its members rose to 23.3 million in 2001, up from about 21 million in 1997.[4]

A majority of the city governments surveyed by the mayors couldn't meet all the requests for food they received. To avoid running out of supplies, two-thirds of the cities reduced the amount of food they made available to individual families, either by cutting the size of each distribution or limiting the number of times people could get help—or both. As a result, the cities left an average 20 percent of need unmet in 2004, up from 14 percent the year before.[5]

Illustrating the diverse face of American hunger, the mayors reported that a majority of people seeking assistance lived in families with children, and a third of adults requesting aid were employed. America's Second Harvest said 40 percent of requests to food banks came from working families.[6] The mayors reported that high housing costs, low-paying jobs, and unemployment, not surprisingly, were the leading causes of the need for assistance.[7]

Although Americans aren't starving, hunger in the United States does injure those who don't get enough of the right food to eat. Hungry children are more likely than well-fed children to be sick, anxious, or depressed. They have a harder time concentrating at school, and they're also more likely to misbehave. Looking closely, we find that some children do poorly in school and get in trouble with the law in part because they don't eat well.

Hungry people and poor people often become hopeless people. That thought occurred to me in Mississippi when Mike Espy told me about one possession nearly all of his impoverished constituents seemed to own—an insurance policy to pay for their burial. From their tiny sources of income, they managed to set aside enough to keep these policies in effect. They wanted to be buried properly, and they didn't want to burden their children with this final expense. They weren't saving for the future so they could live better lives; at a fairly young age, they had begun to save for death.

This seemed to be powerful evidence of their lack of hope. They could scratch together enough money to pay for that burial insurance even while they didn't have enough money to pay for quality food, to improve the sanitary conditions around their houses, or to dress their children in decent clothing. They weren't preparing to live; they were preparing to die.

Yet I also saw here powerful evidence that gave me hope. These poor people were capable of saving. The Grameen Bank's programs to encourage the poor to start savings accounts and to grant them small loans can work in the United States as well as in South Asia, I thought. Here in the poorest parts of Mississippi, I had found more proof for my arguments in favor of American microenterprise. Many people think that tiny loans to the poor or small savings accounts can't put a dent in poverty. But I have seen poor people turn small loans into going businesses that lifted their families to a higher economic status. Over and over again, I have seen tiny steps to help the poor grow into marvelous attacks on hunger and poverty. It's the result, as Mother Teresa said, of doing what's in front of you.

In Washington, for example, I participated in a Wednesday morning prayer group that was formed to follow the biblical instruction to pray for leaders. We prayed not only for national leaders such as the president and members of Congress but also for Washington's mayor and city council members and business leaders and for the benefit of all of Washington. We felt the capital was a special place. It was every American's second city. If you're from Dayton, Washington is your capital. If you're from Sacramento, you may live in the capital city of California, but Washington is your capital too. We all should pray for the leaders of America and the city in which they do their work.

We didn't advertise the group, but it was open to anyone who wanted to attend, and our regular membership was quite diverse. Frequent participants included members of Congress, city officials, business executives, ministers, and local residents of various economic levels, including the poor. For a long time, we met downtown in the city's main public library, which was named for Martin Luther King Jr., a minister whose great civil rights leadership sprang from his faith and from his understanding of God's admonition to serve the poor, the hungry, and the oppressed.

I usually opened the meeting by reading from the Bible. We'd pray. Then a spiritual leader would talk about the lesson in the Scripture. Until his death in 1995, Rev. Sam Hines of the Third Street Church of God usually filled that role. Sam's church took seriously its obligation to serve the poor people who lived all around it, and he could effectively explain how the day's reading related to us and how it related to the city.

Our prayers and discussions inevitably turned to what we should and could do to serve the poor of Washington. Local agencies offered many services, but the people who needed help often didn't know how to get it. So we decided to set up a telephone hotline.

We raised funds to acquire the phone line, and we recruited volunteers to answer the calls. The sick, the homeless, the hungry, people in trouble with the law—anyone who needed help—could call. One of our volunteers would connect the caller with the appropriate agency and stay on the line until it was clear that the caller was getting the assistance needed. We called it the People's House Hotline, and it now has built a database with information about more than thirty-five hundred agencies in the Washington metropolitan area. Today it is operated by the Southeast White House—sometimes called the Little White House—a marvelous institution in Washington's poorest community, which also grew out of our prayer group, as explained below.

In addition to meeting the physical needs of Washington's poor, we prayed about reconciliation in a city very much divided by race, economic status, and partisan politics. We wanted to bring people together, perhaps in a place where they could meet, talk, share meals, and have fellowship. Eventually we raised enough money to purchase a house in Southeast Washington. It's called the Southeast or Little White House because it's on Pennsylvania Avenue (just like the president's house), it's white, and it has columns and other architectural features that suggest the more famous mansion. It's also a name of pointed irony, because the neighborhood around the Southeast White House, at 2901 Pennsylvania Avenue SE, is a world away from the president's digs at 1600 Pennsylvania Avenue NW.

For purposes of assigning addresses, Washington is divided into four sections—Northwest, Northeast, Southwest, and Southeast. The people who run the Southeast White House sometimes refer to Southeast Washington as the "forgotten quadrant," because it is the poorest section of the city, and its residents often feel neglected by better-off Washingtonians. Nearly a quarter of Southeast D.C. residents live in public housing, for example; more than a third qualify for public assistance; and more than three-quarters of the quadrant's children live in single-parent households. Because of its location in this neighborhood, the Southeast White House became not only a place of reconciliation but also a place to serve the poor.

I tell people the Southeast White House was prayed into existence. Not only did the concept spring from our prayer group, but much of the building's renovation was accomplished by volunteers from churches both nearby and far away. I remember one church recruiting a large number of volunteers—including skilled craftsmen—who put in a kitchen, new wiring, new plumbing, and new bathrooms. Other churches donated supplies or money. Several churches have created ongoing relationships with the Southeast White House. Out-of-town churches send youth groups to spend a week or so at the Southeast White House. The young people do volunteer work in inner-city Washington and visit some of D.C.'s tourist attractions. Living and working among Washington's poor, the visiting youngsters learn about the inner city and develop relationships with people they otherwise never would have met. For some of the visitors, this is their first real contact with the poor.

This White House is run by two remarkable men who themselves embody the relationships across superficial boundaries for which we prayed. Sam Morrison is a former Washington policeman. Scott Dimock retired from a private nongovernmental organization. Sam is African-American. Scott is caucasion. They walk together in serving "the least of these." And they have maintained relationship building at the core of what the Southeast White House does.

The short-term visits from out-of-town volunteers, which Sam and Scott call "urban plunges," provide great examples of that principle. So do the many meals this White House hosts. Their "Reconciliation Luncheons" bring together people who would not normally sit around the same meal table—members of Congress, affluent professionals and business executives, poor residents of the neighborhood, suburbanites, people of all races. At weekly breakfasts, men from around the metropolitan area gather for fellowship, prayer, and discussion of how to follow Jesus in the workplace and how to serve as role models for young people, especially for the youths who live in the poor community this White House serves.

The organization's Friends Mentoring Program requires a profound commitment from volunteers and demonstrates that relationships are key to Southeast White House service programs. The program matches first graders with volunteers who each commit to spending at least four hours with their assigned child every week until the child finishes high school. As I write this, more than fifty children have been matched with mentors, and the first mentor has been working with several girls for more than eight years. The similar Sibling Mentoring Program—modeled after Big Brothers Big Sisters—requires volunteers to spend ten hours a month with a child. As with the Friends Mentoring Program, sibling mentors have been paired with about fifty children, and another fifty children are on a waiting list. When mothers saw the effect the mentors were having on their children's friends, they knocked on the door of this White House and begged to have mentors for their kids as well.

Under the direction of a professional tutor, volunteers work one-on-one with students who need help with their schoolwork. The Southeast White House sponsors sports teams and classes in dance as well as in sewing, cooking, and other life skills. Washington artists teach courses in drama,

music, drawing, painting, and ceramics. "Mom's Night Out" regularly scheduled events help young mothers learn parenting and other needed skills.

The Southeast White House's value to the community can be seen in a message
a Fraternal Order of Police leader sent to his fellow police officers. "I urge every
member of the Metropolitan Police Department to consider lending a hand and
a heart to the wonderful programs under way at the Southeast White House,"
wrote G. I. Greene, chairman of the D.C. Metropolitan Police Department Labor
Committee. "I believe we can be excellent mentors to young men and women who
are in real need of responsible adult role models. Isn't it much better to meet them
at the White House instead of the Station House?"[8]

In a very different corner of Washington—the affluent Upper Northwest—
another successful act of reconciliation is symbolized by another renovated
house, this one known as Friendship Place. You can't exactly say this house
was prayed into existence, although neighborhood religious institutions
played a very important role in its creation. It actually grew out of a bitter confrontation—between affluent and poor, black and white, government and citizen—that was reconciled by many neighbors through goodwill.

The conflict began when the D.C. government announced it was going to
open a fifty-bed overnight shelter for homeless men in an abandoned police
station, which was located on a corner shared with a church, a nursery school,
an elementary school, and the edge of a quiet, affluent, white-collar neighborhood of single-family homes. Because there weren't fifty homeless men hang-
ing out in the vicinity of the site, they were to be bused in from other parts of
the city each night and shooed out the door each morning—about the same
time the little children would be arriving at school.

Neighborhood response was frenzied. Nearly one thousand people jammed a
hastily called community meeting at the school, Janney Elementary, overflowing
the gymnasium into the halls and onto the lawn and sidewalks outside. Lawyers
were mobilized. Legal actions were filed. City officials were besieged. And the
government retreated—about twenty blocks south along Wisconsin Avenue, to
Guy Mason Recreation Center, on the edge of another upscale residential area at
the upper end of Washington's famed Georgetown neighborhood.

The local response to the Guy Mason proposal was identical, but this time
Mayor Sharon Pratt Dixon would not retreat. The battle was on—in court,

before the zoning board, and even in the National Park Service, which had participated in the recreation center's development. The mayor, a black woman, was demonized as an amoral politician who was out to boost her standing among poor and minority voters by forcing an unneeded shelter into the city's whitest and most affluent ward. The white and affluent residents of Ward 3 were demonized as racists and elitists who might talk about compassion but wouldn't tolerate social services for the needy near their backyards. The shelter's intended residents were alternately depicted as the innocent victims of a cruel economic system and of heartless rich folk, and as drug- and alcohol-crazed predators who would molest the neighborhood's children, rape the women, and mug the men. A few neighborhood residents spoke out in favor of the shelter proposal, but most expressed a mixture of outrage and fear.

The battle raged for two years. Shelter opponents spent some $100,000 in legal fees. Advocates for the homeless staged a takeover of the recreation center. They even disrupted Easter services at a neighboring church whose congregation opposed the shelter. In the end, once again, the affluent neighbors prevailed, and the mayor let the concept of the Guy Mason shelter fade away.

The issue of helping the homeless in that Northwest Washington community did not end there, however. While nearly all the residents in the area opposed placing a fifty-bed overnight shelter near an elementary school or in a recreation center, some were unsettled by the fury they witnessed among their neighbors. They did have, they believed, some obligation to help the homeless. As early as the immediate aftermath of the raucous meeting at Janney Elementary School, friends began discussing their concerns. Soon—in living rooms, coffee shops, and churches—small clusters of neighbors were independently creating a new movement.

Among those who attended the Janney meeting was Kathleen Partridge, an octogenarian who had reared four children in the house where she still lived about ten blocks away. She found her neighbors' conduct "shameful."

"It wasn't a good location" for a shelter, she agreed, "but people overreacted. They were so angry. When we came out of the meeting, we were so shocked, a few of us. We talked on the phone. We said we ought to do something. We had one small meeting at someone's house. We had another meeting and another and another, and the ranks sort of swelled. I think it was just people calling their friends."

When the conflict shifted to the Guy Mason Center, Jean Duff experienced a similar reaction to the activities of her neighbors. Jean was rearing three- and five-year-old children within two blocks of Guy Mason, and she led a neighborhood organization that was renovating the center's playground. She didn't like the idea of an overnight shelter opening there. She also believed an overnight shelter would do nothing to solve the underlying problems that cause homelessness.

As she became acquainted with a growing number of neighbors who felt strongly on both sides of the dispute (including Mrs. Partridge and her friends), Jean searched for a common ground that didn't involve the Guy Mason shelter. She circulated a proposal to "organize as neighbors to help our homeless neighbors." To try to bridge the neighborhood fissures, she asked Lois Williams, a supporter of the shelter plans, to join in convening a community meeting. Lois, a lawyer who lived near Janney, had represented the homeless in class-action lawsuits that resulted in court orders for shelters to be opened throughout the city. She was active in a committee that advocated the creation of shelter and services for the homeless in Ward 3.

About forty neighbors attended the meeting, which was held at St. Alban's Episcopal Church, about four blocks from Guy Mason. They had represented various sides in the debates over the proposed overnight shelters. Now, Jean told them, they had to put those disputes behind them and find agreement. In the process, she redefined the issue they faced. Throughout the battles over the proposed city shelters, most residents of the nearby neighborhoods saw the question as, how do we stop the government from dumping fifty bums on our doorsteps? Now it was to be, how do we help our homeless neighbors? Although there weren't large numbers of homeless people wandering the streets in this affluent corner of Washington, there were some. And a few of them were quite well known in the community. The neighbors at the meeting decided to create an organization, which they called the Community Council for the Homeless.

This development brought great relief to the area's clergy, who had been deeply troubled by the conflict. They regularly preached God's admonition to serve the poor. Yet most of the members of their congregations were adamantly opposed to the city's shelter plans. Shelter opponents held meetings at St. Columba's Episcopal Church, located across the street from the abandoned police station, and at St. Luke's Methodist Church, located across the street from Guy Mason. Clergy who commuted from the suburbs were attacked as outsiders who had no personal stake in the battle.

Especially concerned because of his church's location, St. Luke's pastor Andrew Gunn invited his fellow Ward 3 clergy to a meeting to discuss the matter. About two dozen attended. A few started thinking about offering shelter in their churches. And that thought meshed with the first plan of the Community Council, which had decided to ask local congregations to consider hosting small shelters.

St. Luke's opened the first shelter, with six beds available year-round. St. Columba's, St. Alban's, Metropolitan United Methodist, and St. Paul's Lutheran followed with shelters that would be open only during the winter months. The Roman Catholic Church of the Annunciation decided to maintain two transitional apartments for the homeless in neighborhood apartment buildings. St. Columba's started what church members called their "water ministry"—washers, dryers, and shower facilities in a corner of the church where the homeless could clean themselves and their clothing.

The churches supplied the facilities, some financial support, and a base of volunteers. But the shelters really were broad community projects, with the Community Council raising additional funds and helping to organize a larger volunteer corps to support the congregations' activities.

Providing more than a bed and a roof, the church-based shelters endeavored to help their residents move toward self-sufficiency. They offered access to counseling and training. The volunteers helped to reconnect the homeless with the broader community by sharing meals at the shelters and developing friendships with the residents.

The majority of those housed at the St. Luke's shelter "have been able to put their lives back together," Gunn says. "When they left us, they had jobs and money in the bank, were self-sufficient, and were able to move back out into the community and become productive citizens."

Thomas Omholt, the pastor at St. Paul's, tells of a shelter resident who became a Sunday school teacher at the church after gaining control over the alcoholism and depression that had driven him into homelessness in the first place. "He's a bright guy who became gainfully employed" in the Washington area's booming high-tech industry, Omholt says.

Despite the success, the council soon concluded that the church-based shelters weren't enough. Council members raised funds to hire a social worker to research the extent of homelessness in the area, listen to what the homeless said they needed, and attempt to link them with help. Then the council decided it needed a facility from which it could coordinate the volunteers and offer such daytime services as counseling and medical care.

Primarily by soliciting religious congregations and obtaining a federal grant, the council was able to purchase a house on Wisconsin Avenue, only about three blocks from Janney School. Randy Denchfield, owner of a suburban roofing company who grew up in the neighborhood, knew that the building trades magazine *Roofing/Siding/Insulation* coordinates a charitable rehabilitation project every year. He brought the Community Council's house to the magazine's attention, and it became that year's project. A local architect did the design for free. About twenty manufacturers donated the construction supplies. About a dozen Washington-area contractors volunteered to perform the work. As a result, the house became the best-looking property along that strip of the avenue. The council christened the facility Friendship Place—to honor the name of the immediate neighborhood, Friendship Heights, and to impart an amiable message to affluent and homeless neighbors alike.

The project was not without conflict. When plans for the facility became public, nearby residents expressed concern, and about eighty-five nearby merchants signed a petition of protest. Council members listened to the complaints and promised to run the facility in a manner that would not disrupt the neighborhood. The building would house the offices of the council's staff and provide social services to the homeless during the day, but it would not become a gathering place for large numbers of the homeless. It would not house an overnight shelter or feeding center. The homeless it served would be told the importance of not creating a neighborhood nuisance.

Today a paid staff of twenty-two runs the council's day-to-day operations, which include a wide range of services for the homeless. Five formerly homeless men or women live with a resident manager in each of three houses, two owned by the council and one by St. Columba's. A dozen formerly homeless people live in apartments managed by the council, some of which the council leases and some of which are leased by area congregations. Four congregations continue to operate small shelters in their churches. St. Columba's still offers its water ministry. A total of twenty-two congregations contribute to the council's work in various fashions. A medical doctor, a nurse, and a psychiatrist see homeless patients at Friendship Place eight hours a week. A social worker, sometimes accompanied by a volunteer, travels the streets at least five days a week and sometimes on weekends, meeting homeless people, building relationships with them, and encouraging them to use the council's services. The organization's newsletter routinely publishes the stories of formerly homeless men and women who turned their lives around with the council's help. Often the stories are written by the formerly homeless themselves.

Over the years, the council has won respect and support from many neighbors and much of the business community. The computer store next door maintained the council's computers for free in the organization's early days and now works on the more complicated computer system at a discounted price. A condominium complex, next door on the other side, provides parking for staff and volunteers. A nearby shop frames the organization's artwork and certificates. A nearby Starbucks keeps the office supplied with coffee. The neighborhood Whole Foods grocery store donates food. The council counts about 250 volunteers, about 30 of whom work every week. Three-quarters of the organization's income is donated by neighbors, and the rest comes from government programs.

And Jack Bubis—who owns a beauty shop a few doors away and was one of the early opponents of Friendship Place—now regularly cuts the hair of one of the neighborhood's longtime homeless men.

"It makes him feel good," Jack says. "It makes me feel good."

He's doing what's in front of him.

CHAPTER 9

RIPPING OUT THE ROOTS OF TERROR

Our Good Works Will Make Us Safer

★ ★ ★

D riving through southern Sudan in 2003, I came upon the remnants of a battle that had taken place ten days earlier. About one hundred vultures were picking over human bones. Some of the skeletons still wore beads and other jewelry around their necks. In what sounded like a tale from some distant past, we were told that horsemen had ridden through the village, cutting everybody down with long swords. The next morning, having contemplated the scene overnight, my traveling companion, Fred Heyn, said, "I felt like we were walking through the valley of the shadow of death."

Sudan's civil war, which has raged for most of the last fifty years, has produced some of the most gruesome scenes I have ever witnessed. In much of southern Sudan, there is little functional modern infrastructure. The people cannot raise enough food to feed themselves or earn money to purchase what they need. Malnutrition is common, and some people starve. There are few educational opportunities and little access to medical care. The fighting has driven more than 4 million refugees from their homes and killed more than 2 million. During just the two years ending in mid-2005, an estimated 180,000 people died, many from hunger and disease; about 2 million were driven from their homes, and 2.3 million needed food aid.

By the time I visited Sudan again in the latter part of 2004, its Darfur region had become infamous around the world as the site of the planet's worst current humanitarian crisis. Accompanying a convoy that was delivering relief supplies, I came to a camp that I was told held more than 115,000 refugees. They had fled their homes to escape the violence of the war. They were terrified to go into their fields for fear of being attacked, murdered, or, in the case of the women, raped. Because of that, they weren't able to plant, so the food shortages continually became worse.

The camp was a desolate place. Under a bright blue sky, reddish-brown sand spread out in all directions, broken only by occasional clumps of weeds and lone trees with no leaves. Men and women wandered about in flowing robes.

But here there also was hope. Under international pressure, led in great measure by the United States, the warring parties had cut back the fighting, and a peace process of sorts seems to be moving forward as I write this about a year later. Tall mounds of food bags, stamped "USA," testified to the United States' leadership in providing humanitarian aid as well as in pushing peace. Nearby, someone was leading a group of children in a chant.

"USA, OK!" they shouted, bright smiles illuminating their dark faces. "USA, OK! USA, OK! USA, OK!"

I firmly believe that these children, and their parents, will remember who came to their aid in their hours of desperate need. Jesus teaches us to feed hungry people—even our enemies. I believe that's also good foreign policy.

The United States boasts not only the world's greatest military but also the world's greatest food basket. That food could be the most important arsenal for our war against terrorism, but we don't use it as effectively as we might. We distribute more food and other humanitarian assistance—by far—than any other nation. Yet in my travels, I have discovered time and again that many of the people who receive our aid don't know where it's coming from. Similarly, Americans have been at the forefront of campaigns to free political prisoners, to stop violence against the weak, and to abolish oppressive systems such as apartheid. Yet in much of the poor and unfree world, our efforts are little known, and we are viewed in a negative light.

We must provide more aid, and we must campaign more frequently and assertively on behalf of freedom. But we also must do a better job of informing those we help about what we're doing for them.

Americans' lack of knowledge about the importance of efforts to fight hunger, poverty, and oppression causes us to do too little—and to take too little credit for what we are able to do. I was intensely frustrated for years because I couldn't convince our foreign-aid agencies to slap our name on the billions of dollars of relief supplies we shipped to the hungry and the poor. I'd see thousands of unlabeled sacks of food stacked in refugee camps or bouncing along in the beds of relief agencies' trucks. I knew they came from the United States, but nothing proclaimed that fact to the recipients. Many international agencies and nongovernmental organizations opposed identifying the supplies with a particular country, and U.S. officials went along.

Finally, our government wised up to the value of a brand, and now "USA" and the American flag proudly announce where those sacks of lifesaving supplies come from. Many bags also declare, in the local language, "Donated by the people of the United States." And this is not short-term advertising of the generosity of the American people. These bags are sturdy and durable. People in these poor countries turn the bags into luggage and use them to carry food. Now when I travel in these places, I see people carrying our flag down their streets, a constant reminder of who helped them in their time of need. I've seen this even in North Korea, where there now are six million U.S. food bags being used for these purposes all over the country.

When we feed hungry people—and help them solve other problems—we create goodwill that can last for generations, cement alliances, and make us safer in an often dangerous world. When it comes to our enemies, if we feed them, we confuse them, soften them, change them. In the long run, it's powerful foreign policy to help people in need, even if we don't get along with them, even if they don't thank us for it right away. Because they will remember.

Proof of this fact can be discovered readily in Europe. More than sixty years after the end of World War II, it's easy today to find Europeans who remember and are grateful for what the United States did then—not just in helping to win the war, but in helping to rebuild the European economies afterward, including those of our enemies.

I'll never forget how Italian prime minister Silvio Berlusconi explained his decision to support the U.S.-led war in Iraq. He said one of the reasons he loves America is our implementation of the Marshall Plan after World War II. He went on television and told his constituents that he wanted Italians never to forget it was the United States that helped rebuild Italy, our World War II enemy, after the war.

I've heard similar statements in many other places over the years, because what the United States did after World War II was so different from what victors traditionally do. We didn't plunder the conquered countryside. We didn't enslave our defeated enemies. We fed the hungry, clothed the naked, healed the sick, and freed the oppressed. We helped them build democracies and rebuild their economies. These actions turned our former enemies into our closest friends. Not one of our current enemies has done to us anything approaching what the Japanese, Germans, and Italians did to us in World War II. Our enemies in World War II tried to conquer the world, and they killed four hundred thousand of our troops in the attempt. Now they are among our most reliable allies.

When we think about enemies, it's also important to remember that we're talking about a relative handful of leaders. Al-Qaeda may claim to represent all of Islam in its campaign of terror against the United States and other nations on its list of enemies. But most Muslims don't want to kill Americans. North Korean dictator Kim Jong Il may rattle nuclear warheads and get himself named by the U.S. government as a member of the international "axis of evil." But most North Koreans don't want conflict with Americans. I know this because I've traveled through so many countries, talked with so many people, seen how they live, and observed many opportunities for America to build goodwill by doing good works.

Even in the "Hermit Kingdom" of North Korea—which I've visited six times—I've seen signs that aid and engagement can win the hearts of the people and command the attention of rulers. Even there, I believe, it's possible to wear down barricades and move toward peace.

Korea's reluctance to deal with Western powers in the mid–nineteenth century first earned it the Hermit Kingdom title. The title has been applied to North Korea for the last half century because of its closed-door policy to most of the rest of the world.

Hearing stories of tremendous deprivation behind North Korea's tall walls of privacy in 1996, I wanted to see for myself. I told North Korea's mission to the United Nations in New York of my desire to visit. I assured them my motive was purely humanitarian, not political. I guess my years of humanitarian travels and advocacy earned me credibility on that point, because the North Koreans surprised me greatly by saying I was welcome to go.

My trip wasn't welcomed by the U.S. government, some of my colleagues in Congress, and some of our allies in Asia, however. Even friends questioned why I would undertake such a mission. They called North Korea an enemy, pointing out that we've never formally concluded a peace treaty to end the Korean War. "Why," they asked, "would you want to help them?"

I told them I wasn't interested in the well-being of the North Korean government; rather, I was interested in the well-being of the North Korean people. There were reports that a million of those people had died already and that most of the victims were children. To those who understood my faith, I pointed out that Jesus told us to feed the hungry. He didn't say he wanted us to feed the hungry except in North Korea. To that, a prominent South Korean pastor simply shrugged his shoulders and said, "You Americans are so naive."

What I discovered during my travels through North Korea is that it probably is the most poorly governed country on earth. South Korea, which evolved slowly into a true democracy during years of prodding by human rights activists—including me—boasts one of the world's most vibrant economies. North Korean dictator Kim Jong Il, who styles himself "Dear Leader," lives in luxury in the capital of Pyongyang, as does his governing elite. They scrape together enough resources to support the fourth-largest army in the world and to mount a serious nuclear weapons program. But ordinary North Koreans are horribly poor, because that totalitarian regime oppresses them, squanders what they have of wealth and income, enforces a dysfunctional Communist economic system that nearly the entire planet has rejected, and prevents them from learning anything from the rest of the world.

Former ruler Kim Il Sung (who called himself "Great Leader") set himself up as god, and his son Kim Jong Il is portrayed as the son of god. No matter where you drive throughout North Korea, you see Dear Ruler's face on billboards. The people are told that he is all-knowing. Because of that, North Korean officials find it next to impossible to admit that they have problems and need help from outside.

Away from the capital, where most of North Korea's few visitors are confined, you feel you've stepped back into a much earlier century. I never saw direct evidence of this myself, but Chinese Buddhists on the Korea-China border told me that North Korean refugees related rumors of cannibalism. Families were said to fear leaving dead bodies unguarded because they might be snatched to be eaten! What I did see was hunger, abject poverty, and a near-complete absence of economic activity. I met people who wore hats, coats, and gloves inside their houses because there was no heat. I saw children eat grass because there was no food. A 1998 study found that 16 percent of North Korea's children were severely malnourished. Among one- to two-year-olds, the figure exceeded 30 percent.[1] I was told that two-thirds of North Korea's children were stunted in growth, that kids who looked at first glance to be eight or nine years old were actually eighteen or nineteen. The malnourishment stunted their mental development as well. The Red Cross tested water at 840 hospitals and found every sample to be contaminated. I saw people washing food and clothing in ditches of clearly contaminated water.

On my first visit, I was astonished at how quiet the countryside was, and how dark at night. There was almost no source of energy, so people couldn't drive vehicles, light buildings, or operate factories. We had to wear heavy coats indoors because of the lack of heat. We traveled for miles without encountering another vehicle on the road because of the lack of gasoline. When we did come upon a car or a truck, it usually was broken down. There was no sound of industry. At night, it was pitch black. Driving through municipalities was like passing through ghost towns. Occasionally I'd see a candle burning in somebody's window, but even that was rare.

More than three-quarters of North Korea is mountainous. The climate is marked by long, cold, dry winters and short, hot, humid summers. Farming here would be a challenge in the best of circumstances. Under the current economic system, it is disastrous. And massive floods made things even worse in 1995.

As I traveled, I noticed that much of the countryside was treeless because the people cut wood to heat their homes and cook their meager food. Because they were hungry, they harvested their crops too early and thereby made their food shortage worse. Because of their isolation, North Korean farmers were kept ignorant of the latest agricultural techniques, so they practiced archaic farming methods. They didn't know how to care for their soil. I once walked into a cornfield where each stalk had produced just a single ear. North Korean officials have admitted that more than a million people died from the famine, but I believe the true number is much higher.

I was amazed initially by the government's willingness to let me visit. My ability to travel around the country compounded the amazement. My handlers—though clearly nervous about my activities—even let me stop the car and walk into villages where I would engage ordinary North Koreans in unscripted conversations. I always take my own interpreter with me on trips like this so that I can be sure I'm communicating clearly. That's how I get the most accurate picture of what's going on.

In one village, I met a woman who didn't have any food in her house and had eaten just one meal in the previous two days. I asked her what she had at that meal. She said a small bowl of gruel.

I saw a girl picking weeds in a park and asked her why. She said, "For food." She was small, emaciated. She looked to be seven years old but told me she was fourteen. I asked her if there was a church nearby I could visit. She said, "There are no churches in North Korea." On another occasion, my handlers tried to prevent me from seeing a little girl who was trying to eat a kernelless corncob. But I noticed her before they ran up to her, slapped the corncob out of her hand, and pushed her away.

In a town on the east coast, I visited a hospital that had no antibiotics, no anesthetics, not even any aspirin. Cotton balls and cloths were drying on the windowsills. They had been washed to be used over and over in the surgery ward. Patients were strapped to operating tables so they could be held still while being operated on without anesthesia. The hospital pharmacy stocked nothing but herbs. I had to wear a heavy coat because there was no heat. There also was no food. Patients could eat only if their families brought food to them. I visited about thirty hospitals during my six trips to North Korea and saw these conditions repeated throughout the country.

I visited many orphanages as well. People told me families took their children to orphanages because they couldn't feed them. Unfortunately, food—along with heat, light, and medicine—was scarce in the orphanages too.

People in authority often didn't tell me the truth, but I frequently was able to check the facts for myself. I had heard that many of the children who lived in orphanages were sick, primarily because of malnutrition. When visiting an orphanage, I'd inevitably be taken to rooms filled with healthy children. But I could always hear kids crying in discomfort in other rooms. At one orphanage I visited, I asked how many sick children were there, and the woman in charge told me thirty. Later I was able to wander about the building on my own, and I counted many more sick kids in rooms I wasn't supposed to see.

I frequently encountered people with stomach problems—some who simply complained of discomfort, others who were doubled over in pain. I discovered that these problems resulted from the government's most desperate attempt to cope with famine—the production of so-called "alternative" or "substitute" food.

Workers gathered weeds, stems, bark, leaves, flowers, and other plant forms and took them to little factories, one of which I was able to visit. In America, this is yard waste that we mulch or compost or put out for the trash trucks to haul away. In these North Korean factories the government had scattered across the country, it was mixed with some grain or soybeans, ground into flour, formed into noodles, and distributed as food. This substance may sate immediate hunger pangs, but the body can't digest it properly; discomfort, diarrhea, and internal bleeding are the frequent result.

I encountered great antagonism to the United States during my first visit. In this closed society, people knew only what their government told them through the state-controlled television, radio, and newspapers. They were told that America is the evil empire. And they were told this from the earliest age. I walked into a school during my first trip and saw a poster that portrayed an American soldier bayoneting North Korean children. The message clearly was "Beware of Americans."

North Korean officials treated me a bit better during my second visit. By my third and fourth trips, they realized I really was there only to help. They thanked me repeatedly for America's food donations. They saw that I hadn't used the trips for any personal political advantage. When I left their country and talked to the media, I never maligned the North Korean government. I wanted to, but I felt there was no purpose in publicly proclaiming how terrible this government was. Plenty of other people were doing that. And biting my tongue allowed me to continue to enter the country to try to help the innocent people there.

After each trip, I reported my findings to my government, to friendly Asian governments, and to the people through the news media. While I didn't malign North Korea's government, I did describe the hunger and poverty I witnessed. I called on our government and our affluent friends to send aid to the North Korean people. I also carried my message to churches in South Korea and to Korean churches in the United States.

At the beginning, this was a very lonely labor. There was so much hatred on all sides. Japan's hatred of North Korea was intense. North Korea hated Japan for atrocities committed during World War II. North Korea's huge military posed an immediate lethal threat to South Korea and to the nearly forty thousand U.S. troops stationed there.

The United States and some of our allies did increase aid to North Koreans. At one point we supplied 80 percent of all food aid sent there. The Japanese remained adamant about not helping, however. By 1999 I had become so frustrated with their position that I conducted a news conference in Tokyo and berated their inaction, something I felt uncomfortable doing.

"Once again I heard the many reasons why the [Japanese] government will do nothing to help, while North Korea's people starve," I said after what I called a "chilling" meeting with government officials. "All of the reasons make political sense. But they are heartless and not at all like the great nation I know Japan to be. I have visited more than one hundred countries and have seen Japan's generosity in extending aid many times. When it comes to North Korea, though, I am convinced that history will not be a kind judge. Japan's stockpile of three to five million tons of rice is slowly rotting, and storing it costs Japan more than the entire UN annual appeal. Meanwhile, two million North Koreans have starved in the worst famine since colonial times."

Someday, I said, when North Korea recovered, North Koreans would remember who didn't help them—especially those countries that were sitting on surpluses they could have given so easily.

Japanese officials didn't like a United States congressman criticizing them in public, but they did send aid.

I didn't envision this as a one-way exchange—our giving to the North Korean people and getting nothing in return. I saw it as a road to peace. The North Korean government's willingness to tolerate my activities helped to convince me that officials there wanted to improve their relationship with the

West and relieve the plight of their people, if only they—and we—could figure out how to do so.

On my last visit, North Korea's leaders made clear that they were desperate for help. Officials—right up to Foreign Minister Paek Nam Sun—begged me to ask President Clinton to visit the country before he left office. They told me, and they told other people, that they were ready to make a deal. They were ready to sign an agreement that would have led to dismantling their nuclear weapons program. It was shortly after our 2000 presidential election, and they didn't know whether they could do business with President-Elect Bush. So they wanted to cut a deal with Clinton.

I stopped in South Korea on my way home, and South Korean president Kim Dae-jung repeated the same message over and over, not letting me leave his office for two and a half hours until he was sure I was convinced. If President Clinton would talk with the North Koreans, he would obtain agreement to reduce the threat from their nuclear weapons, ease tensions along the North-South border, and supply more effective humanitarian aid to the North Korean people, Kim said.

Back in Washington, I requested a meeting with President Clinton and delivered that message to him in the Oval Office. "If you want to win the Nobel Peace Price," I told him, "this is your opportunity." He replied that he had time for just one major initiative in the few remaining weeks of his presidency, and he was focused on trying to bring peace to the Middle East.

Determined to keep pushing, I went to Erskine Bowles, the president's chief of staff, and made my case again. "Forging a lasting peace agreement between Israel and the Palestinians is a noble goal," I told him, "but one unlikely to be achieved in the time left for this administration. You'll get a deal with North Korea. I guarantee they'll lay out the red carpet, and President Clinton will be a hero."

In his memoirs, Clinton wrote that Secretary of State Madeleine Albright made the same argument. She had visited North Korea—a significant sign in itself—and told Clinton the North Koreans were ready to sign an arms agreement. But he stuck with the Middle East and reached no agreement there.

In 2002 Kim Jong Il himself attempted to engage President Bush by sending a written personal message through two well-regarded U.S. foreign policy experts—Donald Gregg, former ambassador to South Korea; and Don

Oberdorfer, former diplomatic correspondent for the *Washington Post*. Gregg and Oberdorfer revealed in mid-2005 that they were given the message while visiting Pyongyang three years earlier. Writing in the *Post*, they said Kim's message was this: "We should be able to find a way to resolve the nuclear issue. If the United States makes a bold decision, we will respond accordingly."[2]

Gregg and Oberdorfer delivered the message. But like Clinton, Bush did not initially respond. Shortly thereafter, North Korea expelled UN weapons inspectors, withdrew from the Nuclear Nonproliferation Treaty, and reopened plutonium production facilities that had been closed as the result of negotiations during the Clinton presidency.

As I write this, North Korea remains hostile, isolated, and heavily armed—and, I am convinced, still desperate for a partner to relieve its isolation. The opportunity still sits there for any American president who chooses to seize it. And glimmers of hope have emerged from the more than two years of negotiations involving the United States, China, Japan, Russia, and both Koreas. I can only hope that by the time you read this book, real progress will have been made toward disarming the Korean peninsula and easing the deprivation of ordinary North Koreans.

I believe opportunities also exist in other unstable corners of the world, where terrorists recruit their irregular armies and plot to kill Americans. In my travels, I've seen that hunger, poverty, and oppression prepare the soil for terrorism. I've seen terrorists recruit new followers by feeding, clothing, and educating them. I've also seen how we can feed and clothe children at schools that teach freedom and love, instead of letting terrorists feed them at schools that teach hate. Such efforts are sowing the seeds of peace and freedom in many conflict-ravaged places. People won't attack you if they view you as their friend. They aren't likely to blow themselves up in suicide attacks if their hearts are filled with hope rather than hatred.

Because of the tremendous difficulty of conducting diplomacy in the Middle East—and the danger posed to people who try to do good there—I have to be circumspect in naming individuals and even identifying places I've visited. When Frank Wolf and I wanted to tour some Palestinian refugee camps, for instance, friends who lived in the region suggested we not let it be known we were American congressmen. If word spread that U.S. government officials were walking around, they said, it might trigger a riot. Our friends arranged for us to be shown around some camps by Palestine Liberation Organization representatives who were told only that we were influential Americans.

At one camp, we found something like forty-five thousand people stuffed into an area of one or two square miles—a population density resembling New York City without anything resembling New York's modern infrastructure. People lived on top of one another in very unappealing conditions. The camp's residents couldn't work outside the camp, and there was no real paying work inside the camp either. The children had few educational opportunities. Open sewers ran along the streets. There was little electricity. The people's lives were unsatisfying, they couldn't strive for anything better, and they came to the understandable conclusion that nobody cared about them.

Articulate preachers of hate thrive in places like this. It's easy to stir up animosity toward scapegoats and then recruit new terrorists.

Frank and I went to the region not only to learn about conditions there but also to talk about reconciliation, using as examples our own relationship and the relationships of others who cooperate across political, religious, and ethnic lines. We spoke to large audiences—mostly of Muslims, but also of Christians and Jews.

One time I met with about thirty young people, both Muslims and Christians, who lived near a Palestinian refugee camp. They asked me, "What are you going to do about the Palestinian question?"

I thought to myself, *What's up with these people, who live inside the Palestinian question, asking me, an American who lives far away, what I'm going to do about it?* So I asked how many of them had visited a Palestinian camp. Not a single hand went up.

I asked them, "Why would you ask me what I'm going to do about the Palestinian question when not one of you has even been in a Palestinian camp? I was in one yesterday."

This incident underscored just how isolated the Palestinian refugees are. Even people who claimed to be their brothers cared so little about them that they had never even bothered to visit a camp. Even next door to the camps, people didn't know what was going on inside the camps and didn't bother to find out. They laid responsibility on others, but the responsibility is theirs too. They should be doing something.

Here's another example: Frank and I became friends with a wealthy fellow who lives in the region and who believes in the need for reconciliation among Muslims, Christians, and Jews. He expressed concern about the plight of the refugees, but he also had never been in a camp. Frank and I took him to one!

He's now involved with a very interesting group of Muslims and Christians who meet for fellowship in the name of Jesus, whom Muslims respect as a great prophet. These people also really care about the refugees and actually are helping. Some of them have great wealth, and some are well connected with political leaders in the region. They feed people, provide athletic equipment, build parks, support education programs, and help train refugees for various occupations. Perhaps most important, they offer some hope to people who don't possess much of that precious commodity.

The United States needs to do more for poor Palestinians and do it more publicly. It's the right thing to do, and it's the kind of thing we must do in our campaign against terror. Hatemongers throughout much of the Muslim world have done an effective job of blaming all problems on Israel, the United States, and other Western countries.

In fact, we do provide aid through the World Food Program, and that helps a lot of Palestinians. But they don't know that it's coming from America, and I think they should know. I also think we should be going inside the camps ourselves, working with the refugees who live there.

I realize the politics of the Middle East makes that difficult. But we need to find ways to let the Palestinians know that we want to be their friends and that we already are helping them. Perhaps we could give more support to non-governmental organizations that aren't clearly identified with the United States and gradually move more Americans in to work there.

There's no doubt in my mind that humanitarian aid is the most effective weapon we can deploy against terrorism—not only because it can make us look good but also because it can alleviate the poverty and despair that breed terrorists. Terrorist organizations such as al-Qaeda use food and education—or rather miseducation—to recruit new terrorists. In their madrassas (religious schools), they use a perverted version of Islam to teach hatred of non-Muslims, justify the indiscriminate murder of innocents, and sanctify suicide bombings. We can use food and education for diametrically opposite purposes.

I met a farmer in Pakistan whose children attended one of those schools. "Why," I asked him, "do you send your children there?"

"First off," he replied, "it's free. Second, they feed my children. I can't afford to send my children to school, because I need them here to work. But if they're fed at the madrassa, I don't have to feed them, so I can afford to send them."

"But they teach hate," I said.

"I know," he said, "but where else am I supposed to send them?"

We need to expand the number of school feeding programs that we support. Governments in poor countries love school feeding because it gets kids back into the public schools. Farmers love it because they save the cost of feeding their children and their kids get educated. Good education fights hunger and poverty by preparing students for better jobs. And these schools can teach peace and respect instead of hate and violence.

To fight terrorists who label us the enemy of the poor and the oppressed, we must make clear that we are the poor and oppressed's best friend.

CHAPTER 10

EVERYONE IS CALLED TO SERVE THE POOR

Learning One
Universal Truth

★ ★ ★

I've traveled throughout the world many times to investigate hunger, poverty, oppression, and other matters of humanitarian concern. Many times I seek public attention during my missions, because my goals often include summoning public action to solve the problems I encounter.

I've also traveled around the world, quietly, for faith. Sometimes these faith-based missions generate more consternation within the American diplomatic corps than the humanitarian missions during which I criticize U.S. policy or seek action by our government when our government doesn't want to act. This is because in a world of many faiths, religion is a sensitive topic from which diplomats flee.

My travels of faith often are made on behalf of the National Prayer Breakfast, which invites people of all faiths from all over the world to pray together in Washington.

During one trip to a predominantly Muslim country—which I can't name because of those sensitivities—my traveling party was briefed upon our arrival by the U.S. ambassador. He seemed extraordinarily nervous about our mission. I surmised he was worried that this group of Americans, headed by an Ohio congressman he didn't know, was going to try to convert Muslim government officials to Christianity and set back the relationship between our countries for a generation. "Be careful when you talk to leaders here about

137

religion," he begged. I told him not to worry. We weren't about to touch off a diplomatic incident.

Accompanied by the uneasy ambassador—who I presume hoped to diffuse disaster should we offend our Muslim hosts—we went off to see the leader of one of the nation's legislative bodies. He turned out to be a gregarious man, full of life. After we had engaged in small talk for a few minutes, he asked me the purpose of our visit to his country. "Our mission is personal, not connected to government diplomacy," I told him. "We're here because of our faith. We want to invite you to our National Prayer Breakfast." In the course of explaining our purpose, I mentioned Jesus in an offhanded fashion. As our ambassador had feared, this had a dramatic effect on the legislator's demeanor—but not in the way our ambassador expected.

This Muslim government leader slapped his leg and exclaimed, "This is amazing! My mother used to talk to me about Jesus. This is one of the most refreshing talks I've had in a long time. To think that you've come all the way around the world from America to talk about something this important. It thrills me to know this. I always thought that Americans were naive and materialistic. None of them talk to me about faith, let alone Jesus. This is wonderful." Then he turned to our ambassador and said, "Why don't you come and talk to me about Jesus?"

I've told this story many times since, and it always gets a great laugh. But it also helps to illustrate two lessons I've learned during my travels.

One is that people of many faiths admire Jesus. His message transcends formal religious boundaries. The Muslim lawmaker's mother would have talked to him about Jesus, for instance, because Islam considers Jesus to be a great prophet. Many Hindus and Buddhists respect his teaching.

Another lesson is that the world's largest faiths all admonish their faithful to feed the hungry, clothe the naked, house the homeless, serve the poor, and make peace. That this admonition often is honored in the breach does not make it less true. This common ground is a place where we can end the horrible religious conflicts that kill so many in the name of God. It's also where we can join together to rid the world of hunger, poverty, and oppression, as God clearly wants us to. Thankfully, millions of Jews, Christians, Muslims, Hindus, Buddhists, and others are doing just that.

The Judeo-Christian Scriptures—both the Old and New Testaments—are jam-packed with references to the poor. And there's no mistaking what God commands us to do—not only through his words but through the very way Jesus lived his life. One of Jesus's first great miracles was to feed the multitude in the desert. He helped strangers. He touched lepers. He loved everybody. Asked once which is the greatest commandment, Jesus replied that it is to love God. And the second, he added, is to "'love your neighbor as yourself.' There is no other commandment greater than these" (Mark 12:31).

One of Jesus's most memorable prophecies is about how he will reward the righteous on Judgment Day for having fed him when he was hungry, given him drink when he was thirsty, welcomed him when he was a stranger, clothed him when he was naked, and visited him while he was in prison. When the righteous express puzzlement, not remembering having done those things for him, Jesus will explain that when they did kindness to "the least of these," they also "did it to me" (Matthew 25:40). "When you give a banquet," he taught at another time, "invite the poor, the crippled, the lame, and the blind. And you will be blessed, because they cannot repay you" (Luke 14:13–14). And Paul told the Corinthians that "God loves a cheerful giver" (2 Corinthians 9:7).

God was delivering this message long before Jesus's birth. In Proverbs, Solomon declares, "Whoever is kind to the poor lends to the LORD, and will be repaid in full" (19:17). It is the only way we are told we can lend to God, who usually is giving to us. Solomon also warns, "Whoever gives to the poor will lack nothing, but one who turns a blind eye will get many a curse" (Proverbs 28:27). In Deuteronomy, God commands his people, "Open your hand to the poor and needy neighbor in your land" (15:11). Isaiah admonishes us to "learn to do good; seek justice, rescue the oppressed, defend the orphan, plead for the widow" (1:17).

More than two thousand verses in the Bible deal with the poor. In my travels, I've seen thousands of Christians and Jews serving the poor in some of the world's most difficult places. I've also learned of Muslims, Hindus, Buddhists, and people of other faiths who help the least of their brethren.

When I paid my first visit to Ethiopia during the catastrophic 1984 famine, I found World Vision and the Missionaries of Charity laboring heroically to supply food and medical treatment to an overwhelming mass of starving people.

One of the largest Christian relief and development organizations, World Vision has been providing emergency aid, education, health care, and economic development assistance since 1950. Mother Teresa founded the Missionaries of Charity in India that same year to love and care for the poorest of the poor and the sickest of the sick, whom no one else was helping. Like World Vision, Mother Teresa's missionaries now work on every populated continent.

You've probably heard of other prominent Christian organizations that follow Jesus's instruction to serve the poor—Catholic Relief Services, the Salvation Army, Habitat for Humanity, and Bread for the World, to name just a few. There are many such groups, large and small. And thousands of individual congregations do their part—perhaps by operating their own soup kitchen or homeless shelter, or by volunteering to help in community organizations, or by donating money that can be put to use anywhere in the world.

A national survey coordinated by the Hartford Seminary in Connecticut in 1999 and 2000 found that the vast majority of American congregations did such service. About 85 percent supported a food pantry or soup kitchen. The same proportion gave cash assistance to needy families or individuals. More than half supported thrift stores. A third supported housing programs.[1] A similar survey found that more than nine in ten American mosques gave cash to the needy, and about two-thirds supported soup kitchens and collection drives for the poor.[2]

Two-thirds of America's emergency food providers are faith-based organizations.[3] And faith-based groups were prominent in the efforts to help victims of Hurricane Katrina in the American Southeast in 2005.

The Union for Reform Judaism activated its disaster relief fund, as it always does in such times, and quickly raised $2 million. In conjunction with the town of Utica, Mississippi, where the union has a camp, it opened a distribution center for relief supplies. Reform Jews across North America collected food and other supplies and shipped them to the camp. Volunteers lived at the camp and helped to staff the distribution center.

For two decades, American Jewish World Service has operated relief and development projects throughout the third world. MAZON: A Jewish Response to Hunger supports antihunger efforts around the world with $3 million in annual contributions from American Jews.[4]

One of the most effective humanitarian organizations in history, the Grameen Bank, which I write about in detail in chapter 3, was founded by a Muslim, Muhammad Yunus. It makes tiny loans to the poorest of the poor so they can create or expand their own tiny businesses. This remarkable enterprise was born in the mid-1970s when Yunus, an economics professor at Chittagong University in Bangladesh, loaned $27 to forty-two craftspeople and saw them begin to pull themselves out of poverty.[5]

In Bangladesh today, the Grameen Bank has more than fifteen hundred branches, fourteen thousand employees, and 4.75 million borrowers in thirty-seven thousand villages. The borrowers repay their loans 99 percent of the time.[6] I became so impressed with Grameen's accomplishments that I worked to bring microlending to the U.S. government's overseas aid efforts and to programs that help the poor within the United States itself. Now, lenders that are affiliated with Grameen, or simply copy Grameen's methods, operate in about sixty countries, including prosperous nations with a minority of poor citizens, such as the United States, Canada, France, the Netherlands, and Norway.

"If I could be useful to another human being, even for a day, that would be a great thing," Yunus has said. "It would be greater than all the big thoughts I could have at the university."[7]

Buddhist monk Sukho Choi, also known as Venerable Pomnyun Sunim, has been laboring for years in a cause dear to my heart—providing aid to the hungry, poor, and oppressed people of North Korea. (I tell you about my six visits to the so-called Hermit Kingdom in chapter 9.) This is particularly noteworthy because Choi is South Korean, and North Korea is his country's mortal enemy.

Informing his fellow South Koreans that more North Koreans have died from famine than perished in the Korean War, Choi has raised millions of dollars and thousands of articles of clothing to feed and clothe the needy north of the 38th parallel. Choi and his followers pressure the South Korean government to offer humanitarian aid to people in the north, and they urge other nations and international relief groups to do so as well. Choi founded several organizations that do humanitarian work in North Korea and India, help North Korean refugees in South Korea and China, and provide emergency relief when it's needed in various parts of the world. His actions demonstrate that you don't have to be a Christian to act in accordance with Jesus's instruction to feed your enemy.

People of different faiths also are joining together in humanitarian efforts, sometimes in very difficult circumstances. In 2004 the Ramon Magsaysay Award for Peace and International Understanding—which often is referred to as the Asian Nobel Peace Prize—was given to a Muslim and a Hindu who have reached across the India-Pakistan border, working to ease long-standing animosities between their two populous and nuclear-armed nations.

Ibn Abdur Rehman, a Muslim born in the Indian state of Punjab in 1930, was forced to move to Pakistan with his family after Britain partitioned its Indian colony into the independent countries of predominantly Hindu India and predominantly Muslim Pakistan in 1947. In adulthood he became a prominent journalist, eventually rising to edit the *Pakistan Times*. Laxminarayan Ramdas, the Hindu, became a military officer and capped his distinguished career as the Indian navy's chief of staff.

In 1994, having retired from their journalistic and military careers, Rehman and Ramdas helped to create the Pakistan-India Peoples' Forum for Peace and Democracy. The group fosters dialogue between Indians and Pakistanis from all walks of life, to build understanding among residents of nations that have fought several wars and are engaged in a perpetually smoldering, religion-fueled conflict over who rules Kashmir, a predominantly Muslim state on the Indian side of the Pakistan-India border. In addition to organizing meetings on both sides of the border, the forum has lobbied both governments to ease travel restrictions between the two countries and to remove the demonizing of the other side that appears in both countries' schoolbooks.

In accepting their award, Rehman and Ramdas both discussed a fact of human relationships that I discovered in Congress and during my travels in various parts of the world: it is easier to resolve differences—and harder to demonize others—if you really get to know the guys on the other side.

Rehman said that even when the Indian and Pakistani governments conclude formal peace agreements, "the bitterness and prejudice of centuries cannot be washed away by state protocols only." Needed, he said, are many experiences like one described by an Indian teacher who led students on a visit across the border. There the students "discovered a Pakistan that was quite different from what they had read about in their history books." Ramdas agreed that "getting the youth of both countries together has been a great achievement." The face-to-face discussions that occur during such visits are "chiseling away some of the prejudices" and helping to "lift some of the myths that had earlier been treated as gospel," he said. A decade into the forum's work, Ramdas said, "I am happy to say that we are a healthy and vibrant lot."[8]

In the Balkans, a corner of Europe riven with bloody ethnic and religious conflicts, a Christian mission brings together young adults of differing faiths to lay the groundwork for long-term reconciliation. Since 1999 the Renewing Our Minds conference has been conducted by Life Center International in Fuzine, Croatia, a beautiful town near mountains and lakes that is popular with tourists. Young people ages eighteen to thirty—primarily from the Balkans but also from other places plagued by conflict—spend three weeks in this peaceful setting, just a half hour from the Adriatic coast, getting to know one another and finding the common ground beneath their differences.

Stevo Dereta, a Baptist minister who helped to found the conference, came to the conclusion that reconciliation in the Balkans had to begin with the young. The participants arrive bearing the identities that have divided the Balkans for centuries—Albanian, Bosnian, Croat, Serb, Montenegrin, Macedonian, Slovene, Roman Catholic, Orthodox, Muslim, Protestant. Conference leaders do not ask non-Christians to convert, but the program is based on the teachings of Jesus. Participants first study Jesus and the Gospels, then examine their communities' conflicts, and finally learn about reconciliation. Follow-up programs and reunions support the participants after they return home.

The project intends to grow "a new generation of leaders eager to work towards building peace and reconciliation," in the words of Tihomir Kukolja, director of Renewing Our Minds and Life Center International.[9] He has collected testimony from participants who offer evidence that the effort may succeed. The conference "made me realize that God is one and the same for all of us," a Macedonian woman said. An Armenian man predicted that "the results of the friendships built at [the conference] will bring great changes, from forgiveness to conflict resolution."

Many people are reaching across religious boundaries within the United States as well. Often this occurs as Christians realize they have much in common with members of other denominations, despite disagreements that result in some of us calling ourselves Baptists, Presbyterians, and so forth. The Hartford Seminary study found that 7 percent of U.S. congregations were engaged in service projects with people of different faiths. A third of the congregations were working with members of different denominations.[10]

Among the most-talked-about recent events has been the decision of the National Association of Evangelicals to issue a statement titled "For the Health of the Nation: An Evangelical Call to Civic Responsibility." While evangelical churches have long carried out projects to help the disadvantaged, the association has tended to take conservative positions on public policy and to focus its political efforts primarily on issues of personal morality, such as abortion or same-sex marriage, as its fifty-two member denominations and related organizations also tend to do. By unanimously adopting this call in October 2004, however, the association's board endorsed government action to aid the poor, both at home and abroad, and to protect the environment.

"We call all Christians to a renewed political engagement that aims to protect the vulnerable and poor, to guard the sanctity of human life, to further racial reconciliation and justice, to renew the family, to care for creation, and to promote justice, freedom, and peace for all," the association declared. This includes "advocating for effective government programs and structural changes." While evangelicals will disagree about some political issues, the association acknowledged, "We have many callings and commitments in common: commitments to the protection and well-being of families and children, of the poor, the sick, the disabled, and the unborn, of the persecuted and oppressed, and of the rest of the created order."[11]

Though the Bible does not require economic equality, the association affirmed that the Bible, "condemns gross disparities in opportunity and outcome that cause suffering and perpetuate poverty, and it calls us to work toward equality of opportunity. God wants every person and family to have access to productive resources so that if they act responsibly they can care for their economic needs and be dignified members of their community."[12]

The association called on Christian politicians to "shape wise laws pertaining to the creation of wealth, wages, education, taxation, immigration, health care, and social welfare that will protect those trapped in poverty and empower the poor to improve their circumstances." It advocated making reduction of global poverty "a central concern of American foreign policy." And it proclaimed that "government has an obligation to protect its citizens from the effects of environmental degradation."[13]

God gave humans "a sacred responsibility to steward the earth and not a license to abuse the creation of which we are a part," the association declared. "Our uses of the earth must be designed to conserve and renew the earth rather than to deplete or destroy it. We urge Christians to shape their personal lives in creation-friendly ways: practicing effective recycling, conserving resources, and experiencing the joy of contact with nature. We urge government to encourage fuel efficiency, reduce pollution, encourage sustainable use of natural resources, and provide for the proper care of wildlife and their natural habitats."[14]

With few exceptions, this is a platform that could be embraced by the liberal activists who traditionally view evangelical Christians as natural political enemies—and by people of all faiths. "On issues like poverty, the cold war among religious groups is over," Rev. Richard Cizik, the association's vice president for public policy, told the *Washington Post*.[15] "I think this rallying cry for the poor may be one of the issues that can let evangelicals, Roman Catholics and mainline Protestants work together," he said in another interview with the *Christian Post*.[16]

No wonder, then, that Cizik was among scores of religious leaders and hundreds of rank-and-file believers who showed up for an interfaith convocation on hunger at Washington's National Cathedral in June 2005. Muslims, Buddhists, Sikhs, Jews, and all manner of Christians convened in the Episcopal cathedral to call for an end to hunger.

Addressing the gathering, Rev. Njongonkulu W. H. Ndungane, Anglican archbishop of Cape Town, South Africa, suggested that the event spoke to more than hunger.

"Perhaps we should learn the lesson that when we talk about doctrine and the abstract concepts of faith, we find far too many reasons to disagree," he said. "But when we put our faith into practice, look what we can achieve together."[17]

There's no doubt about it. Jesus, after all, did not establish the Anglican Church, the Baptist Church, the Roman Catholic Church, or the Greek Orthodox Church. Jesus simply said, "Follow me."

CHAPTER 11

THE DEMOCRATIC PARTY

Finding Common
Ground within
Our Political Family

$\star \; \star \; \star$

I didn't pay much attention to politics while I was growing up. My parents were registered Republicans, but really they were inherently nonpartisan—or bipartisan. They had as many Democratic friends as Republican friends. When the discussion around our family dinner table turned to public affairs, my parents never spoke with a partisan slant.

My dad didn't graduate from high school, but he was a smart man and a hard worker. He started a laundry business and made it successful. After I left home to attend Denison University near Columbus, Dad won a seat on the City Commission in Dayton, a predominantly Democratic city, then became mayor. His party affiliation didn't matter much because Dayton had a nonpartisan government and party labels didn't appear on the ballot.

Throughout high school and college, my big interest was sports, and I was good enough at football to become a Little All-American running back at Denison. Like so many people of my generation, however, I did get caught up a bit in the Kennedy mystique.

John and Bobby Kennedy and their extended families were young and vibrant and had ideas and great vision and were making things happen. They weren't afraid to take chances. They created things, such as the Peace Corps. They called on young Americans to serve, and many responded—including me. I have to confess, though, that my motivations for joining the Peace Corps weren't entirely altruistic. I did want to do good, but I also was looking for adventure. And I thought it would be fun to see close-up a part of the world I didn't know anything about.

I was sent to teach English in Thailand, and that became a real wake-up call. I'd never been around poverty before. Now I was living in the midst of it, in a strange country, halfway around the world from where I had spent my entire life up to that point. It was mind-boggling just to discover that the little things we take for granted in the United States were beyond the reach of the Thais among whom I lived. All my life, if I became thirsty, all I had to do was turn on a faucet, fill a glass, and take a drink. When I was dirty, I stepped into a shower, turned on a faucet, and washed myself thoroughly under a stream of warm water. If you drank tap water in Thailand in the 1960s—where you could find it—you'd likely get very sick. Where I lived, you bathed outside by the well, contorting inside a kind of loose robe for privacy.

I returned to Dayton after about two years as a much more mature young man. The experience taught me not only about poverty but also about taking care of myself in a situation that was foreign to me. I was motivated to continue to do good, but I didn't have any clear path in mind. I started to settle into the real estate business. Then the Montgomery County Democratic Party asked me to run for the state legislature.

The Democrats thought I could be an attractive candidate. At the time, Dad was very popular as the Republican mayor of Dayton. Democratic Party leaders figured he could help me raise campaign contributions and reassure Republicans that it would be OK to vote for me. Both of my brothers were popular too. Mike had played football for Fairmont High School. Sam had won the silver medal for diving at the 1960 Olympics and had served one term as a state representative. I was fairly well known around Dayton in my own right because of my high school and college football career. I had roots in both Dayton, because of Dad's public office, and the adjacent suburb of Kettering, where my family lived until I went off to college.

The question was, was I really a Democrat? And the answer was yes. My parents' lack of strong partisanship was one factor. More important was the pull of the Kennedys, which my experience in the Peace Corps strengthened. It's hard for today's young people to understand, but politics was viewed as an honorable and exhilarating endeavor in the 1960s.

It's amazing how little I knew about public policy when I entered that first campaign in 1968. Even though the Vietnam War was tearing apart the country—and especially the Democratic Party—I focused on a few state and local issues in my race for the Ohio House of Representatives. I won, as the party leaders had anticipated, but initially I didn't make much of an impact in Columbus, the state capital. For my first two years in office, I pretty much kept my mouth shut and tried to figure out how the system worked.

People who know me today would find it hard to believe, but I was quite shy then. I was very nervous when speaking in front of groups. That natural inclination to remain silent was reinforced by the best political advice my dad ever gave me.

When I was recruited to run, I asked Dad about it.

"I'm young, I don't have any political experience, and there are so many things I don't know," I told him. "What am I going to do when somebody asks me about something I don't know anything about?"

"Tell them you don't know," he replied, "then go find the answer."

After I won election to my second term in 1970, I decided I was ready to start spreading my wings, speaking out on issues and taking stands. I became deeply involved in mental health, mental retardation, and environmental protection, which were really big issues at the time. An estimated twenty million Americans turned out for the first Earth Day in 1970. Ohio had become notorious for warehousing the mentally ill—and too often people who were misdiagnosed as mentally ill—in huge institutions. Reformers were trying to move those who weren't mentally ill into more appropriate living situations and to place those who were sick in treatment programs that really worked. Although Richard Nixon had won the White House for Republicans the year I won my first election, Democrats were on the rise in Ohio, capturing the governor's mansion and most other elected executive offices in 1970, the Ohio House in 1972, and both legislative chambers in 1974. Even though Republican Jim Rhodes took back the governor's seat in 1974, it remained an exciting time to be an Ohio Democrat.

I moved up to the Ohio Senate in 1973. Then Charles Whalen, the beloved moderate Republican who had been Dayton's congressman for six terms, announced he would not seek reelection in 1978, and I ran for his seat.

That congressional race was the only time I can honestly say I really enjoyed a campaign. The Republicans nominated a classy, smart, strong candidate—Dudley Kircher, president of the Dayton Area Chamber of Commerce. He ran as a classic urban Republican, and I was pretty much a textbook urban Midwestern Democrat. We held numerous debates, and we focused our campaigns for the most part on real issues. I think the main reason I won was that I addressed the major concerns of what then was the traditional core of the Democratic Party—blue-collar workers, Catholics, African-Americans, the poor, and the middle class. They comprised a majority of the Third Congressional District, so I won the election.

At the time, I was pro-choice. I had always felt uncomfortable with my position, but I also had always bought into the notion that a woman has the right to make up her own mind. Initially, this caused trouble for me with some longtime Democratic voters in my district, especially some Catholics. They constantly pushed me, and they became angry with me when I would not change my position. The harder they tried to push their issue—their faith—down my throat, the more stubborn I became. Later, after I changed my position, I remembered that experience as a lesson about the fact that you can't force your faith onto someone else.

A few years after I arrived in Congress, I began to come to and grow in faith. After much study and prayer, I decided that I had to oppose abortion because of my new conviction that the fetus is a child who matters to God. The media, of course, noticed—and reported—when I started to cast pro-life votes. Many pro-choice Democrats felt betrayed, and my name became mud in their circles. I noticed that some people who had been supporters and friends, when they saw me walking down the street toward them, actually would turn and walk the other way.

By this time I had held elected office for about fifteen years and had built a strong, positive personal relationship with my constituents. Most either didn't care very much about abortion, already were pro-life themselves, or were willing to accept my change on that issue because they agreed with me on so much else. Local Democratic Party leaders accepted my new position because they knew me, understood me, agreed with me on most things, and knew that on the core values of our party, I was going to keep winning.

Those leaders were right. I had no problem winning reelection in my congressional district. When I finally left Congress in 2002, I had been elected to twelve terms, more than anyone else in the history of the Third District. I knew I had to give up any thought of running for higher office, however. It was extremely unlikely that a pro-life candidate could win the Democratic Party nomination for governor or senator in Ohio, and it was unthinkable that a pro-life candidate could find a place on the national ticket. As time went on, I experienced another phenomenon—people who shared my faith but couldn't understand my politics.

Politicians of all stripes learn to shrug off disparagement of our occupation. Otherwise, we would risk becoming perpetually furious about the jokes told at our expense. Making fun of politics and government has been America's national pastime for much of our history. I doubt that Mark Twain was the first commentator to sink his barbs into public officeholders. But he was quite adept at it, writing back in the nineteenth century that "it probably could be shown by facts and figures that there is no distinctly native American criminal class except Congress."

I discovered, however, that as a man of faith, I'm subject to a special form of this traditional harassment. On more than one occasion, I was introduced to an audience as "a Christian and a congressman," then had to smile through gritted teeth as people giggled at this improbability. Once, in a church, an old fellow sitting near the front shouted, "Make up your mind, buddy! You can't be both."

The fact that I'm a Democrat elicits yet another variety of incredulity, this time often quite serious. I've stopped counting the number of times I've been asked how I can be a Democrat and a Christian. Usually I try to deflect the question with humor. "A lot of Republicans," I say, "are going to be surprised when they get to heaven—*if* they get to heaven—by all the Democrats they see walking around up there." Or I point out that when Jesus entered Jerusalem, he wasn't riding on an elephant!

Humor aside, these attitudes illustrate a serious problem for the Democratic Party. Democrats—particularly at the national level—have allowed themselves to become viewed not only as a secular party but as a party that is hostile to faith. A 2005 survey by the Pew Forum and the Pew Research Center found that a majority of Americans view the Republican Party as friendly toward religion, while less than a third feel that way about Democrats, for example. Interestingly, nearly half of Americans say nonreligious liberals have too much control over the Democratic Party, and the same proportion say religious conservatives have too much influence on Republicans.[1]

The poll also showed why this is so significant. Eighty-one percent of Americans believe in God. Religion is very important to 60 percent and somewhat important to an additional 25 percent.[2]

Our party is not antifaith. But complaining won't do us any good. We've allowed ourselves to slip into this current hole. Now we have to find a way to climb out.

This has happened in part because of how cleverly the Republicans have been able to exploit our weaknesses. They have very publicly embraced people of faith, especially more conservative people of faith, while the Democrats at times have shunned opportunities to embrace people of faith. Republicans have set Democrats up to appear to be the antifaith party by engineering votes and running campaigns about symbols of faith—such as organized prayer in school or displays of the Ten Commandments in government buildings—which Democrats, who tend to be strong supporters of the separation of church and state, are apt to oppose. They have even managed to contrive campaigns that make Democrats appear to be proponents of same-sex marriage, although as far as I can tell, most Democrats aren't.

But Democrats have contributed to their own problems. Many Democratic public officials and candidates are uncomfortable talking about faith. This is not a moral failing. Like me, they believe it is better to show a sermon than to speak one. They worry about being labeled hypocrites, because so many politicians have misused faith for their own partisan purposes. They believe faith is a private thing. But Republicans have stepped into this vacuum and convinced many believers that they are the party of faith and we aren't.

Democrats also have let themselves be defined as the party of abortion. Absolute support for the right to abortion in all circumstances has become so important to party activists that many people perceive that it is our most important issue. It is a litmus test for national office, and that's true in many states as well.

There was a time when Republicans let themselves appear to be the narrow, intolerant party. That perception helped send GOP nominee Barry Goldwater to a landslide loss in the 1964 presidential election. Because of the rising importance of abortion, however, Democrats became the narrow, intolerant party in much of the 1980s and 1990s. This unfortunate development became particularly obvious when Bob Casey, the pro-life Democratic governor of Pennsylvania, was prevented from speaking at the Democratic National Convention in 1992. Except for abortion, he was a solid traditional Democrat who focused on the needs of the poor, the blue-collar workers, and the middle class. Former Democrats who are pro-life still cite that as a reason for switching allegiances.

After Bill Clinton won the 1992 presidential election—in part because Republicans let intolerant extremists steal much thunder at their convention—I began working to insert a "conscience clause" in the next Democratic Party platform. The idea was to acknowledge that pro-life Democrats have a place in the party, even if the majority of party leaders are pro-choice. About forty pro-life Democrats in the House campaigned for this clause. President Clinton—a smart politician—understood the value of the big tent and supported our proposal.

In August 1996, during my first visit to North Korea, I was wakened by a phone call in the middle of the night from George Stephanopoulos, then a top Clinton aide. I was sleepy and befuddled and asked "George who?" when he introduced himself. "Tony," he said, "the president wants you to speak at the national convention in Chicago about the conscience clause you put into the platform." The North Koreans were tapping all of my phone conversations, of course. They must have thought I was somebody pretty special to get a call from the White House. I wondered if they had any idea what a conscience clause is!

I had quite the journey from famine-plagued, oppressed North Korea to the podium at the convention of the world's oldest democratic (small *d*) political party in just a few days. When I climbed onto the high stage and surveyed the large hall, I felt an important change was beginning to take place in my party.

"I'm a pro-life Democrat," I declared. "I'm one of about forty pro-life Democrats in the Congress, and many of us have felt left out by our party's position on abortion for many years. But this year is different. For the first time, the Democratic Party has included in our platform a conscience clause on this divisive issue."

I told these mostly pro-choice Democrats about the issues that were closest to my heart: "the needs of the vulnerable in our nation—the poor, the sick, the elderly, the children, and the unborn." I reminded them of Hubert Humphrey's proclamation that "the moral test of government is how that government treats those that are in the dawn of life, the children; those who are in the twilight of life, the elderly; and those who are in the shadows of life, the sick."

I talked about my experiences working among the poor and the hungry. I expressed my pride as a Democrat that our party supports government programs to aid the neediest and volunteers to work in private humanitarian organizations. I told how the Democratic Party in Dayton had opened its headquarters to shelter and feed homeless and hungry families.

"By doing this," I said, "we are showing that Democrats stand for more than just winning elections. We stand for helping people. We Democrats believe that our government, and our whole society, will be judged on how we treat the least of these among us." By adopting the conscience clause, I said, our party had reclaimed its status as "the party where every American can feel welcome and at home."

The clause declared that "the Democratic Party is a party of inclusion. We respect the individual conscience of each American on this difficult issue, and we welcome all our members to participate at every level of our party."

The clause was an important step, but only a step. Party leaders were so worried about pro-choice delegates' reactions to my speech that they went throughout the hall shortly beforehand, telling everyone to treat me with respect and not to boo. When I was introduced, I was greeted by polite applause. When I finished, I heard no more than a few isolated hands clapping.

I spoke again at the 2000 convention in Los Angeles, as did Bob Casey's sons. (He had died earlier in 2000.) That year's platform recognized that Democrats "have deeply held and sometimes differing views on issues of personal conscience like abortion and capital punishment" and described this diversity "as a source of strength, not as a sign of weakness."

As an ambassador, I couldn't take part in partisan politics in 2004, so I couldn't speak at the convention. But the Democratic platform again contained a conscience clause, this time noting that "members of our party have deeply held and differing views on some matters of conscience and faith. We view diversity of views as a source of strength, and we welcome into our ranks all Americans who seek to build a stronger America. We are committed to resolving our differences in a spirit of civility, hope, and mutual respect." In another important step, Senate Democrats chose pro-life Harry Reid of Nevada to be their leader. As I write this, Bob Casey Jr. is the leading candidate for the 2006 Democratic U.S. Senate nomination in Pennsylvania, having been recruited into the race by the very pro-choice Senator Charles Schumer of New York, the chairman of the Democratic Senatorial Campaign Committee.

Democrats lost the 2000 and 2004 presidential elections, and Republicans currently control both chambers of Congress as well as the White House. Following the 2004 election, political analysts focused a great deal of attention on so-called values voters. The assumption was that these were people of faith and that they were conservative. Exit polls showed that one of the clearest predictors of voting preference is how often a voter attends religious services. Frequent worshipers voted for President Bush. Infrequent worshipers supported John Kerry, the Democratic presidential nominee.

These findings should give Democratic leaders pause. But they should not lead us to believe that people of faith won't vote for Democrats. We need to do several things, in my opinion. We need to engage people of faith and treat them with a level of respect that many Democratic activists have disdained in recent years. We also need to remind people of faith that there is more to being faithful in religion than opposing abortion and same-sex marriage. We must not concede the values voters to our opponents. Instead, we need to demonstrate how the Democratic Party advances the values that these voters should support. This is not a hard sell. A 2005 survey by the *National Catholic Reporter* found, for instance, that 84 percent of U.S. Catholics believe helping the poor is a very important Catholic teaching. The only other Catholic belief called very important by the same percentage was Jesus's resurrection.[3]

If you read the Bible, you'll learn that you can't be faithful to the teachings of Jesus without feeding the hungry, clothing the naked, housing the homeless, comforting the afflicted, healing the sick, befriending the stranger, and serving the poor. I've looked hard, but I've never found any passage of Scripture commanding tax cuts for the rich. I differ with most national leaders of my party on abortion and some of the other so-called social issues. But we agree on much more. And I believe in focusing on agreement.

The trouble is that many Democratic activists haven't paid attention to their agreements with me—and with the many other people like me. They have publicly focused on what separates us, and the squeaky wheel has gotten most of the attention from the party leadership. I've felt marginalized by my party, as have many former Democratic voters who could become Democratic voters again if their concerns are listened to and they are treated with respect. It's time for party leaders to embrace these other common values with as much will and enthusiasm as they have shown for choice in regard to abortion. It's time to stop abandoning those who agree on so many important issues other than abortion. It's time pro-choice Democrats reach out to pro-life Democrats and say, "Let's work together on those issues. Let's elect candidates who will serve the poor and make peace—who will focus on the middle class instead of the rich."

Jim Wallis, evangelical activist and author, tells a wonderful story about meeting at Notre Dame University with Catholic activists who complained that the Democratic Party didn't respect them. One young woman said, "Four thousand unborn lives were lost today [to abortion]. How can I vote on anything else?" Then a young man said, "Well, nine thousand died today because of HIV/AIDS." Then another activist remarked, "Thirty thousand children died today because of utterly curable diseases, lack of food, and clean drinking water."[4]

There is plenty we can work on together, and we don't have to abandon important principles in order to do that. I can continue to work to end abortion, and they can continue to promote choice. We can work together on everything else—including reducing the demand for abortion—as long as we respect one another. *Compromise* is not a dirty word in politics. In fact, this kind of compromise is absolutely essential.

One way we can work together to reduce abortion is to reduce the number of unwanted pregnancies. I've learned from my work in the third world that education is the most effective form of birth control. In poor countries with no reliable social security system, people want to have many children who will take care of them in their old age. If the child mortality rate is high, parents want to have even more children so enough will be likely to survive. If we educate mothers about breast-feeding, water purification, proper nutrition, and ways to keep their children healthy, more children will survive and parents won't feel the need to produce so many to begin with. If we also teach reading, writing, ways to earn money, and the wise management of finances, parents won't have to rely on their children so much for old-age security. Population growth will go down, the national economy will go up, and the people will live healthier, happier, and more prosperous lives.

Education works in the United States too. We need to teach girls and young women that having children out of wedlock and before they're capable of caring for them is a ticket to a life of poverty. We need to teach them about birth control and make it available to the poor. We need to teach them the kinds of skills that will enable them to grow up, get good jobs, and become parents when they're truly prepared for parenthood. In addition, we can work together to make adoption easier and to help young mothers cope with pregnancy and early parenthood.

It's also essential to seize those things we agree upon and exert real leadership again. Before Ronald Reagan won the White House in 1980, conservatives frequently complained that Republican politicians were just lightweight Democrats. If Democrats proposed spending a certain amount of money on a government program, Republicans would respond by proposing to spend just a little bit less. Democrats drove the public debate. Republicans always played defense.

Now Democratic officeholders and candidates look too much like lightweight Republicans. Republicans propose massive tax cuts for the rich, and Democrats say, "Let's not cut them quite so much." Democrats are neither yes nor no. They're kind of a definite maybe. And the people in the country who would vote Democratic are not quite sure what we stand for. Now it's the Democratic Party that plays defense.

I blame a lot of this on the enormous cost of campaigns and the enormous influence of rich individuals and special-interest groups that pay the cost. Democratic candidates have come to rely on the same kind of wealthy campaign contributors that Republicans do, so they feel pressure to support Republican-like policies. They've become timid about standing up for traditional Democratic policies that benefit the poor and the middle class. As a result, poor and middle-class Americans feel that they have no real influence on the government—that it doesn't matter which party wins the elections— so many of them don't even bother to vote.

If Democrats are ever to take control of the government again, we have to prove that we deserve to govern by putting forth bold, visionary proposals that will be true to our heritage as Democrats and will enable us to show the values voters that we represent the values they should support. We need innovative ideas that will capture people's imaginations and address their real concerns.

I've observed over the years that the rich do a pretty good job of taking care of themselves. What we need is a lot of people who are committed to taking care of the poor, the middle class, and the blue-collar workers. That's what the Democratic Party traditionally has stood for, and we need to make clear that we continue to do so.

So let's just say flat out that the rich don't need any more tax cuts. Let's proudly advocate policies that will end hunger in America, put the unemployed to work, protect the good jobs of the middle class, preserve the environment, diversify our sources of energy, and make sure all Americans get the health care they need. Let's accept the responsibility of paying for the government services we want and not pass along a big debt for our children, our grandchildren, and their grandchildren to pay. And let's push for real campaign finance reform so that a rich business executive or a special-interest group can't buy a stronger voice in government than a factory worker or a custodian.

The Democratic Party has been playing defense for too long and has lost much of the opportunity to define the debate for mainstream Americans. I remember some good political advice I picked up in football: always have a good offense. In politics, when you play offense you leave the other guy only two choices. Either he agrees with you, and you win; or he disagrees, but you're still defining the debate. Let's tell people who we are and what we believe in. When our opponents contend that government is always the problem and never the solution, let's not hesitate to point out all the great things Democratic governments have accomplished, such as Social Security, Medicare, civil rights, women's rights, workers' rights, minimum wage, and environmental protection.

To start winning again, we need candidates and party leaders who lead.

Americans are looking for leaders, not politicians who wait to see which way the wind blows and which way the polls go. I speak frequently to groups of young people, and I know this is particularly true of them. They are primed for a leader to call them to a good cause, and they will respond. Democrats did well among young voters in the 2004 election, and we can do even better in the future.

It may seem odd that as a Democrat, I accepted the invitation to work as an ambassador for a conservative Republican president. But my acceptance of the position just stemmed naturally from my belief in focusing on agreement. While I disagree with many of President Bush's policies, I have found him to be a strong supporter of important humanitarian work I care deeply about.

He has done a very good job helping the poorest and the most vulnerable people in the third world. He proposed tripling the budget for fighting HIV/AIDS in Africa. He more than doubled humanitarian aid to the poorest countries and helped cancel the debt of fifty of the poorest. During the Bush administration, the United States has become by far the largest donor to developing nations.

When President Bush commissioned me as ambassador, he said, "Tony, I want you to put into action America's commitment to alleviate hunger and build hope in the world." That's the biggest job assignment I've ever had, and I believe the president has put his money where his mouth is in helping me carry out that assignment. That accomplishment surpasses partisan politics.

One of the keys to the president's success in elections has been the public's perception that he speaks plainly about what he believes. Even people who disagree with his policies respect that trait. If Democrats are going to start winning presidential elections again, our candidates have to learn to do the same.

They have to speak clearly and boldly about things that matter. They need to tell the truth, be sincere, and be comfortable in their own skin. I don't think you have to profess a specific kind of faith to win over the values voters. But I think you have to be comfortable in whatever you do say. I don't think it's a coincidence that the only Democrats to win presidential elections in the last fifty years are Jimmy Carter, perhaps the most devout president in our history, and Bill Clinton, who, despite personal sins that became so very public, was always at ease in discussing his faith. We all are sinners, after all.

I would never be the first to inject faith into a political campaign. But we must not cede faith to the other side. If someone says people of faith can't vote for a Democratic candidate because he's pro-choice, that candidate must be ready to insist that all of the other issues be examined too. He has to be able to say that his faith commands him to feed the hungry, serve the poor, protect the environment that God created, and nurture children after they're born. These are moral issues. These are values. This is what government must do to serve "the least of these."

CHAPTER 12

WHERE WE ARE TODAY

Noteworthy Progress but Still a Long Way to Go

★ ★ ★

O ne evening in the fall of 2003, after a very difficult day traveling through the Democratic Republic of the Congo, I sat down for dinner at a restaurant in Kinshasa, the capital. I was tired. I was disturbed by the hardships I'd seen and the stories of atrocities I'd heard that day. I was trying to relax and restore myself for the equally disturbing work I would have to do the next morning.

A young American woman walked up and introduced herself. When she started talking, I was not the least bit unhappy that she had interrupted my meal.

"You're the congressman who sponsored the legislation on conflict diamonds, aren't you?" she asked. I nodded yes. "I want you to know that I'm here as a result of that," she continued. "I've been assigned to the Congo to help implement the Kimberley Process."

What a gratifying moment this was. For several years, Frank Wolf and I had campaigned to end the trade in so-called conflict or blood diamonds, which financed much of the warfare that ravaged the Congo and other African nations— and even helped to bankroll al-Qaeda. The Kimberley Process was the scheme that had finally been adopted to bring this insidious trade under control. And this young woman was flesh-and-blood evidence of our ultimate success.

When you do what I do, you really feed off instances like this. The problems of hunger, poverty, and oppression are so enormous and so resistant to solution that you're always in danger of feeling overwhelmed. To meet this young woman, who was able to help solve a problem because of something Frank and I were a part of, was a powerful antidote to any temptation to give up. Fortunately, even amid the enormous troubles of Africa, there are enough such moments to keep me enthused about this work.

When people ask me if I find this work depressing, I tell them of times I've gone home in the evening, knowing I'd helped to feed thousands of people that day. I sleep well on nights like that. To those who worry these problems can't be solved, I point out that when I returned from Ethiopia in 1984, forty thousand people around the world were dying from hunger every day. Now it's twenty-five thousand. That's still an enormous number. But it would be many thousands more if people weren't out there working hard to ease the suffering.

Two activist groups told Frank and me about blood diamonds in 1999. Especially in Angola, Sierra Leone, and the Congo, warring factions were seizing control of mines and selling the diamonds to finance their armies. For a time, al-Qaeda purchased illicit African diamonds because their high value and small size made them easy to smuggle to various parts of the world where they could then be resold to finance terrorist operations.

The trade in blood diamonds was insidious because as those diamonds worked their way through the marketplace, they blended invisibly with the diamonds that had been produced by legitimate businesses. When diamonds showed up in jewelry stores, customers couldn't tell the difference. An American who purchased an engagement ring as a symbol of love had no way of knowing that the purchase was helping to finance cruelty, death, and destruction.

Al-Qaeda's involvement made blood diamonds a direct threat to the people of the United States and others who were terrorists' targets. In Africa, blood diamonds financed unspeakable atrocities on a daily basis. So Frank and I joined the international campaign to bring this trade to an end.

In Congress, we introduced legislation to require that all diamonds imported into the United States be tracked from the mine. Only diamonds certified as coming from legitimate sources could be sold here. We considered this a modest, reasonable requirement. Many other products sold in America carry labels that tell where they come from. If you can find out where wine or cheese or clothing is produced, why shouldn't you be able to learn where diamonds originate?

We also met with diamond dealers and jewelers, asking them to determine where their gems came from and to refuse to deal in blood diamonds. We added our voices to demands that international organizations forge agreements to stop the global blood-diamond traffic. As I mentioned earlier, we got Martin Sheen to cut an ad about the issue, which aired on the NBC television network after an episode of *The West Wing*. We staged protests in front of Tiffany and Cartier stores in New York. We even ended up being interviewed for a comprehensive, well-written story about blood diamonds that was published in an unexpected place—the *National Enquirer*.

This project took us to the absolute economic extremes of the earth. In London, I visited the headquarters of De Beers, the largest diamond dealer in the world, which once controlled 90 percent of the entire planet's diamond supply. De Beers officials led me on an incredible tour. We passed through rooms full of long tables that were covered with piles of raw diamonds. I saw millions of raw diamonds, tons of diamonds. They were like pebbles on a beach. A De Beers executive put four rough diamonds in the palm of my hand and said they probably were worth about $16 million.

In Africa, we saw what the blood diamonds financed. Warlords, who had launched their evil careers by commanding ragtag guerrilla bands of a few hundred fighters, used profits from the diamond trade to build armies with thousands of uniformed, heavily armed troops. These were not well-disciplined soldiers but amoral sadists who employed unspeakable cruelty to terrorize the people. Their strategy was to rule through fear.

Warfare in Sierra Leone killed tens of thousands, a third of them younger than five years old, and drove more than two million from their homes, many of whom left the country entirely. The rebels spread terror by slicing hands and arms off civilians and hacking others to death. Thousands of girls and young women were abducted, raped, and turned into sex slaves for the soldiers. As farmers fled their lands, they lost their ability to grow food, so malnutrition soared.

Frank and I visited refugee camps where we met children as well as adults whose hands and ears had been cut off. They told us stories of rebels capturing civilians and instructing the captives to choose which extremity they would lose. Others described being forced to reach into a bag and draw out a piece of paper containing a picture of a body part, which immediately would be hacked off. One man told us rebels gave him the choice of losing both of his hands or having his two children killed. He chose, of course, to lose his hands. And after the rebels sliced them off, they killed his children anyway.

In Sierra Leone and Angola, rebels fought government soldiers for control of the country and its mineral resources. In the Congo, a half dozen other nations sent in troops to seize control of diamond mines and loot the Congo's resources. Blood diamonds were both motivating and financing the warfare.

The United States had enormous power to disrupt this trade because Americans purchase about two-thirds of all diamonds sold in the world each year. We could strike a major blow simply by stopping our own purchases. Because of our importance to the diamond market, we could apply effective pressure on other countries and on the diamond industry itself.

Diamond industry executives initially told us it would be impossible to track raw diamonds, and they opposed our calls for action. We introduced legislation anyway. And representatives of diamond-producing countries and the industry, prodded by humanitarian activist groups, met in Kimberley, South Africa, to discuss what they could do. By 2001 we were able to introduce a bill, the Clean Diamonds Act, that was supported by humanitarian groups and the industry.

Congress finally approved legislation in 2003, after I had left the House. Also that year, the talks in Kimberley produced what came to be known as the Kimberley Process Certification Scheme, a mechanism for keeping blood diamonds out of international trade. The United Nations began imposing sanctions on diamond-producing countries that didn't keep blood diamonds off the market.

The blood diamonds story provides a good example of how you have to go about trying to measure progress in the world's poorest places. (Measuring with statistics is tricky, although we must use them. It's hard to gather statistical information in such spots, so different researchers can come up with different numbers. And, of course, they change over time.) Small gains should be celebrated. Comprehensive solutions take a long time. Efforts by so many individuals, organizations, and governments reduced the traffic in blood diamonds and thus cut the flow of funds to warlords and terrorists. But the problem is not solved.

In mid-2005, Global Witness and Partnership Africa Canada, the two activist groups that brought blood diamonds to Frank's and my attention, released a report saying that "considerable progress has been made" but "the Kimberley Process still has a long way to go."[1]

Diamonds continue to finance some fighting in the Democratic Republic of the Congo and the Ivory Coast, the groups said, even though both countries signed the Kimberley agreement. The organizations said the United States needed to publish better data about its diamond trade.

If I were to set foot in the Congo for the first time today, I'd think it was a horrible mess. And it is. But you can detect some signs of progress even there.

From the mid-1960s to the mid-1990s, Mobutu Sese Seko ruled the Congo— which he renamed Zaire—with increasing brutality, and he stole everything he could grab. With support from Rwanda and Uganda, the Congo rebels overthrew Mobutu in 1997. Fighting, which included participation by armies from a half dozen neighboring countries, continued until the last of the foreign soldiers officially withdrew from the Congo in 2003. An estimated 3.5 million died during that time from war, famine, and disease. At least two million more were driven from their homes.[2] Despite the official end to the war, conflict continues in the eastern Congo, with the purported continuing participation of foreign troops. And the entire country will suffer for many years from the effects of lengthy warfare, theft, and the disruption of all aspects of the economy.

The country's transportation system lies in ruins. Travel is further disrupted by countless land mines left over from the warfare. Per capita income is only about $100 a year. Life expectancy is forty-nine years.[3] Bandits roam the countryside, and people are afraid to return to their homes. Many Congolese lost much more than a place to live.

Traveling around the Congo, I met hundreds of girls and women who had been raped—many violently by multiple assailants. The crimes were so brutal that they required corrective surgery as well as psychological counseling.

The Congo's warlords also distinguished themselves by forcing some thirty thousand children—more than a third of them girls—to take up arms. I met child soldiers who were eight years old, wore camouflage uniforms, and had carried assault rifles into battle. They looked lost and scared and mean. They appeared as if their very lives—certainly their childhoods—had been snuffed out of them.

They had been plucked from their homes, given guns, and immediately ordered to kill someone—perhaps a neighbor or a friend. If they didn't kill, they were told, their entire family would be killed instead. So they immediately became killers and assumed the status of both victims and victimizers.

Now these child soldiers and rape victims suffer the additional pain of being rejected by their families and communities. Many parents associate rape with shame and refuse to let raped daughters return home. Many communities fear child soldiers and want them to stay away.

The signs of hope in this unfortunate place are small but significant.

The CIA categorizes the Congo's current government as a dictatorship that is "presumably undergoing a transition to representative government."[4] Our State Department credits Congo president Joseph Kabila with making significant progress toward freedom. The government is working with the World Bank and the International Monetary Fund to repair its broken economy. And the Congo has vast natural resources—both minerals and fertile land—that could support a booming economy if the country acquires effective leadership. Inflation fell from more than 500 percent in 2000 to about 7 percent in 2003. Exports jumped by two-thirds from 2002 to 2004, according to estimates by the International Monetary Fund.[5]

The United States, the World Food Program, and other agencies and countries are helping humanitarian organizations address the difficult problems of individual victims. They offer food, lodging, and counseling to the former child soldiers to help them reclaim lives as normal children. They provide medical care and counseling to the raped girls and women.

As I have throughout the world, I encountered some remarkable individuals doing what's in front of them in the Congo. One example, I have to confess with chagrin, I almost passed up the opportunity to see.

Jay Nash, of the U.S. Agency for International Development, helped to guide me during one of my visits to the Congo. He kept asking me to visit a project he was running during his time off, using his own money. I was busy and tired and distracted and really didn't want to add one more task to my schedule. But he was so persistent that finally I agreed. And I'm so glad I did.

Children still contract polio in the Congo. When they do, it's almost always a sentence to a lifetime of abject poverty and begging. Their parents can't afford to buy them prostheses or wheelchairs. They can't find employment. They get around by crawling or slithering on the ground like serpents. They sit or lie on the ground, and they beg.

Jay bought two houses in a compound in Kinshasa. He went to a junkyard and bought some scrap metal. He created a little workshop in his compound. He recruited a couple of kids with polio and taught them how to build simple leg braces from the scrap metal. When he brought me to see his compound, there must have been one hundred children and young adults in the yard, almost all of them wearing leg braces, a bunch of them playing soccer, others singing and dancing. It was incredible. I thought, *He has literally put these kids on their feet!*

Some of these kids were homeless. He gave them a safe, loving place to live. He taught them a valuable skill. They make braces for themselves and for others. Because they're mobile, they can get out into the community and get jobs. Some of the young adults now work full-time in Jay's shop.

I'm not the only person who has been impressed by Jay's work. I came across a story in the *Philadelphia Inquirer* about NBA star Dikembe Mutombo, a Congo native, visiting the compound and immediately pledging to donate $1,000 a month to the project.

I can tell stories like that about most of the countries I've visited. In many places, such as in the Congo, the stories are part of a bigger picture of a country slowly getting better.

Sierra Leone, for instance, has now become a functioning democracy. More than five hundred thousand people have returned to their homes there. Because the farmers are getting back on their land, rice production has risen to 86 percent of the prewar level.[6] Children are going back to school.

The country remains desperately poor even though, like the Congo, it contains great wealth in natural resources. The resources, tragically, have not been developed for the advantage of the people. One result of the Kimberley Process is to move the diamond trade away from the hands of smugglers and toward legitimate markets that can benefit the country as a whole. Sierra Leone currently has a per capita income of just $150 a year, a life expectancy of thirty-four years, and the highest infant mortality rate in the world, 16.6 percent.[7] It once was known for education, trade, arts, crafts, and well-managed businesses. If violence and corruption can be kept at bay, there's no reason this country can't reclaim that legacy. But it won't happen tomorrow.

Angola, the third country so horribly terrorized by blood diamonds, has been at peace since 2002, except in the Cabinda province to the northeast. Our State Department describes the government there as nominally democratic. President Jose Eduardo dos Santos promised that elections would be held sometime in 2006. Primarily because of its oil deposits, Angola's economy has been growing recently.

A quarter century of civil war levied a horrendous toll, however. Up to 1.5 million Angolans died, and more than 5 million were driven from their homes. Once, Angola exported agricultural products. Now two-thirds of its people survive on subsistence farming, and the country imports about half its food. Life expectancy is less than forty-seven years.[8] Hospitals lack medicine. Schools lack books.

When I search for good news in these places, I seize on two things. One is the big picture—whether fewer people are poor, hungry, and oppressed; whether the government is moving toward democracy; whether there is evidence of growing economic activity. The other is whether I come across people who are doing what's in front of them, making life better in some particular place. People like Jay Nash.

If I focused only on the big picture and not on the individual rays of hope, it would be hard to remain optimistic. There are so many ups and downs, so many steps back to erase the steps forward.

The number of people dying from hunger each day has dropped by more than a third over the last two decades, and that's an unmistakable sign of progress. Between 1970 and 1997, the number of malnourished people throughout the world fell to 791 million from 959 million. That was more good news. However, since then, the world's hungry population has climbed back to more than 850 million, in large part because of the many troubles in Africa.[9]

Nearly 19 percent of the planet's population—1.2 billion people—earn less than a dollar a day. In West Africa, 60 percent of the people live at that income level, and throughout Africa it's about 46 percent. One in five Africans earns less than fifty cents a day. Of the thirty-seven nations with the lowest life expectancy on earth, thirty-six are in Africa. (The other is Afghanistan.) In southern Africa, 40 percent of the population—35.7 million people—undernourished. Africa is the only continent that has become poorer over the last twenty-five years.[10] Drought has damaged crops in various African regions in recent years. Swarms of locusts made things even worse in West Africa. But people—particularly cruel, greedy, or incompetent leaders—often cause the worst tragedies. Africans have a saying: When elephants fight, the grass dies. They see the truth of that aphorism every time warlords field their armies and civilians suffer worse than the soldiers. But bad leaders can destroy a country even without taking it to war, and that's what's happening in Zimbabwe.

Zimbabwe used to be the breadbasket of southern Africa. Now it's a basket case. Once an exporter of agricultural products, it now has to import food and accept donations of food that it can't afford to buy. What once was one of Africa's wealthiest and most productive economies has contracted by a third since 2000. Unemployment is around 70 percent. Inflation ranged between 300 and 600 percent in 2004. In 1998 it took twenty-four Zimbabwean dollars to buy one U.S. dollar. In late 2005 it took twenty-five thousand. In 1980 the average Zimbabwean could expect to live more than sixty-five years. Now life expectancy is less than forty years. A quarter of Zimbabwe's adult population has AIDS at a time when the country's health-care system is collapsing.[11]

Drought and flooding contributed to Zimbabwe's agricultural and economic decline, but it's largely man-made and avoidable. The man is Robert Mugabe, Zimbabwe's president, who has been guilty of corruption, human rights violations, and the implementation of policies that just don't make sense. The country's food shortage stems in large part from Mugabe's decision in 2000 to seize land from competent white farmers and give it to cronies and supporters who knew nothing about farming. In mid-2005, under the guise of "urban renewal" or "cleanup," he turned his wrath on poor black Africans, destroying shantytowns and leaving the former residents with no place to live or to work. Some seven hundred thousand people lost their homes or their jobs.[12] All this is happening in a country with valuable mineral deposits, fertile soil, and a deteriorating infrastructure that is still better than what is found in most of Africa.

I visited Zimbabwe in August 2005 in connection with a shipment of U.S. food relief. As I traveled around to observe some of the country's problems, I met a large number of families shortly after they had been driven off their land. They told me they had documents that proved their ownership. But policemen took the documents, tore them up, and chased away the rightful property owners.

I visited a feeding center operated by Africare Zimbabwe, a nongovernmental relief organization that the U.S. government funds. I tried to visit Hopely Farm, near the capital of Harare, a military-run camp where several thousand people have been living since their homes were destroyed in the "cleanup" campaign. The authorities wouldn't let me in. I was told in a hushed tone that the government didn't want me to see the place because old people were dying there.

We're feeding the people of Zimbabwe under our policy of not letting politics interfere with humanitarian work. But Mugabe makes that work difficult. The World Food Program estimated that 4.3 million Zimbabweans needed food aid in 2005.[13] Government red tape delays delivery of food to the country and its distribution to those who need it. And Mugabe is anything but grateful for this assistance.

Two months after my Zimbabwe trip, Mugabe came to Rome to attend the celebration of the UN Food and Agriculture Organization's sixtieth anniversary. I sat in the audience. Mugabe was allowed to speak.

Instead of thanking us for the aid, he labeled President Bush and British Prime Minister Tony Blair "international terrorists" and likened them to Adolf Hitler. He called me an "agent of imperialism." It was an outrageous performance at an event that was supposed to draw attention to hunger and encourage all nations to do more to help the poor. But that's what we've come to expect from Mugabe.

Thankfully, I've observed progress in places that have suffered even worse than Zimbabwe has.

I felt as if I had arrived at the gates of hell when I traveled to the Tanzania-Rwanda border while genocide was being perpetrated in Rwanda in 1994. The mountains above the Kagera River, which separates the two countries, were breathtaking in their beauty. The scene along the river was as ugly as anything I had ever encountered. Bloated corpses swirled in the river current. Bodies got hung up on rocks and moved in an eerie fashion with the flow of the water. *How is it possible that this could be done by human beings to other human beings?* I wondered.

I struggled to describe the scene adequately to people back in the United States. "Can you imagine visiting something as beautiful as Niagara Falls, only to realize with horror that you're seeing rotting corpses floating in the water below?" I asked. "This is not a modern war. It's a feudal war. People are being hacked to death with machetes, one by one."

Longtime animosities between Rwanda's two major ethnic groups—Hutus, who comprise 85 percent of the population; and Tutsis, who make up 14 percent—fueled the genocide. In just three months, vicious Hutu militias killed eight hundred thousand Tutsis and moderate Hutus who wanted to avoid the clash. Two million Rwandans were driven out of the country, and another million fled their homes for safer places inside the country. After the fighting ended, Rwandans were scattered around their country and in neighboring Tanzania, Burundi, and the Congo. During my trip to the border, I saw three hundred thousand refugees at a single camp in Tanzania. In their panicked flights, husbands became separated from their wives, parents from their children.

When I returned to the region on a later trip, I encountered a remarkable program run by the Irish humanitarian organization Concern. In caring for refugees, Concern's workers noticed how many were separated from their families. The workers became particularly distressed about the many parentless children in their care. They suspected that many of these kids were not really orphans but had living parents someplace else in Rwanda or a neighboring country. Some of these children were so young and in so much shock that they couldn't tell the Concern workers what their names were, where they had come from, who their parents were, or whether they had any idea where their parents might be.

Concern recruited local mothers who could relate to the children. The mothers would spend time with the children every day, talk with them, try to draw out information about them and their families. They'd try to get the kids to remember their names, nicknames, how old they were, what region they had lived in, what city, what town. They asked the kids what their parents looked like, what their names were. They found out whether there were particular toys the children liked to play with, particular things they liked to do. They took photos of the kids and posted them in markets all around the country, along with whatever information they had been able to elicit about the children and their families. And they had tremendous success.

I went with some workers and a child on an excursion into the mountains where they had circulated the child's picture. The child's parents, who had fled to a mountain village to escape the violence raging around their old family home, saw the picture and identified him. When we got to the village, the Concern workers participated in one of the most exciting and rewarding moments they will ever experience. Just witnessing it tore my heart out. These parents had literally run for their lives—run for miles to escape the brutality being visited upon their neighbors. In the horrific chaos, the child had been separated from his mother and father. Now these humanitarian workers were reuniting the child, who didn't think he'd ever see his parents again, with his mother and father, who believed their child was dead.

This was difficult work. Concern workers had to recruit mothers who were willing to spend a great deal of time with these kids. Then they had to distribute information about the children around a primitive country with poor roads and little in the way of modern telecommunications. To a great extent, the information had to circulate by word of mouth. But when I saw them bring a family back together, it was hard to imagine any accomplishment that could be more important.

Rwanda remains a desperately poor country, but it is possible to detect progress here.

The challenges are obvious, starting with the continuing trials of people accused in the genocide and the need to reconcile Tutsis and Hutus into lasting peaceful coexistence. Clashes persist among Tutsis, Hutus, and other ethnic groups along the borders between Burundi, Uganda, the Democratic Republic of the Congo, and Rwanda. Rwanda has the unwelcome distinction of being both predominantly rural and the most densely populated country in Africa. Nine of ten Rwandans depend on subsistence farming for their livelihood. More than a third of the population is undernourished. Annual per capita income is $206; life expectancy is less than forty-seven years.[14]

Hope for Rwanda's future builds upon the international community's commendable, though horribly late, response to the genocide. Too late to save the eight hundred thousand killed, the United States and other countries mobilized an enormous relief effort following the genocide, and the United Nations deployed an effective peacekeeping force. Most refugees returned to Rwanda. An elected president and legislature now run the government. Corruption and crime are relatively low. The government is implementing economic reforms and is working to build an effective educational system and improve health-care programs. Crop yields are rising as more effective agricultural techniques are being adopted.

The place I always look the hardest for hope is Ethiopia, where I discovered my life's mission in 1984. And I always find hope abounding in an isolated place called Yetebon, about ninety miles south of the capital of Addis Ababa. It's there that Marta Gabre-Tsadick and her husband, Demeke Tekle-Wold, have turned absolutely nothing into the most complete private relief and development project I've ever seen.

As I discussed briefly earlier, Marta and Demeke fled Ethiopia when Communist rebels overthrew Emperor Haile Selassie in 1974. They settled as refugees in Indiana where in 1977 they founded Project Mercy with Rev. Charles Dickinson and his wife, Fran. While Marta and Demeke lived in the United States, Project Mercy offered relief and relocation assistance to African refugees. After the Communists were overthrown in 1991, Marta and Demeke returned to Ethiopia and began their work at Yetebon, a poor rural community of about seventy thousand. They do all their work with private funding, most of it raised in the United States.

When Marta and Demeke arrived, Yetebon had essentially no public facilities. On my first visit, I was struck by how they seemed to be living in the middle of nowhere. The area looked as though it might have some promise for agriculture, because the vegetation was green. The fields were surrounded by fairly big hills. There were trees, but I wouldn't really call it a forest. Except for the uncertain rain, the weather there was perfect. Yetebon lies near the equator, but it has a fairly high elevation, so temperatures year-round tend to range from comfortably cool at night to 75 or 80 degrees during the day.

The first thing Marta and Demeke did was build a school, starting with first graders and gradually increasing the scope into high school. Children from all over the region were invited to attend, some walking three, four, even five miles a day to do so. I've watched the kids arrive in the morning, many of them barefoot. The teachers instruct these children in more than the three Rs. They teach healthy habits, cleanliness, the importance of washing their hands after going to the bathroom. If kids arrive dirty, they have to shower and put on clean clothes. They also receive two nourishing meals each day.

Next, Marta and Demeke started an agricultural project, bringing in experts from Ethiopia and the United States to teach the local farmers how to grow a greater variety of crops and how to apply better techniques to increase their yields. In a country often short of water, they ran pipes into the hills above their land to carry water from mountain springs down to the farmland. They dug a well.

Marta and Demeke are remarkably successful at recruiting help—not just donations but knowledgeable volunteers, mostly from America but also from elsewhere around the world. They've built and staffed their facilities with volunteer schoolteachers, high-tech workers, carpenters, bakers, cooks, sanitation experts, health-care professionals, and experts in the latest farming techniques.

They put up a state-of-the-art hospital—probably better than any hospital in Addis. Donors gave them all the equipment. Doctors and nurses volunteer to treat the patients.

Project Mercy once fed 250,000 people during a drought. But its primary goal is to help the people of Yetebon become self-sufficient. That's why, in addition to school classes for children, there are courses for adults in carpentry, metalworking, basket making, embroidery, spinning, and other useful skills—as well as a day-care center so both mothers and fathers can become educated and hold gainful employment.

These skills are being put to use in the construction of beautiful residential neighborhoods. The houses are simple but solid. They have indoor plumbing with hot and cold running water—something unheard of in the past. Local carpenters build the houses' furniture.

Marta and Demeke are Christians working in a predominantly Muslim community, and early on that led to tensions. But I've met Muslim leaders in the area, and now they praise and thank these two Christians for the good they've done for the community.

Compared to most of Ethiopia, Marta and Demeke have created paradise.

Ethiopia is far better off today than when I first visited the country two decades ago, but it still has a long way to go. The people enjoy more freedom than Ethiopia has ever known, but the government doesn't meet our standards for liberty and democracy. Annual per capita income is just $116, and life expectancy is forty-nine years.[15]

When I visited in 2004 and 2005, I still encountered mothers who had to walk hours to feeding centers to get nutritious food for their underweight babies. Particularly because of AIDS, I met young orphans who were caring for even younger siblings.

While Ethiopia no longer faces mass starvation—and the government wouldn't try to hide a need for assistance—about a tenth of the population still regularly requires food assistance. And that number can double when unfavorable weather leads to low crop yields.

The key, of course, is to do as Marta and Demeke do and help Ethiopians become able to fend for themselves. That is now the Ethiopian government's policy. In dramatic contrast to the Ethiopian regime of 1984, which refused to admit the extent of famine during the great drought, the current government has acknowledged the severity of hunger there and has formed a coalition for food security with donor nations, UN agencies, and nongovernmental humanitarian organizations.

I witnessed the impact of that approach when a group of farmers showed me through fields where they were learning how to apply modern agricultural techniques to grow a wider variety of vegetables to nourish their families and to sell for cash. They were feeding themselves, and they were proud that they were able to do so.

There are days when what I do doesn't seem to produce even that drop in the ocean that Mother Teresa talked about. But then I'll discover a place where a piece of legislation I sponsored is having a concrete effect on reducing the suffering of war, as I did when I encountered that young woman in Kinshasa who was working to end the trade in blood diamonds. Or I'll meet people who, on a small scale, make individuals' lives more worth living, as I did when Jay Nash showed me how he helps polio victims in that same city, and as I do each time I visit Marta and Demeke in Yetebon. Or I'll explore sites where organizations I support are distributing food that is keeping people alive in an emergency while also helping them learn to become self-sufficient in the future.

At times like that, I remember that what I do—what they do—saves lives and makes lives better, and that in the long run there really is hope. And I think to myself, *This is not a bad day. I'll sleep pretty good tonight.*

CHAPTER 13

NEW ORLEANS

America Discovers Its Invisible Poor

* * *

I didn't witness firsthand the tragedy that Hurricane Katrina visited upon New Orleans at the end of August 2005. I was in Rome, as the U.S. ambassador to the UN food and agricultural agencies that are headquartered there. So, like most of the world, I watched my television set in horror as the hurricane spread destruction across parts of Louisiana, Mississippi, and Alabama, then left tens of thousands of people to fend for themselves in the cruel aftermath.

Unlike most of my fellow viewers, however, I knew exactly why the calamity unfolded as it did. And I knew there quickly would be a counterflood of help from throughout the United States.

Hurricane Katrina revealed two important truths about America. The first is that our poor are invisible, so most Americans don't even realize they're there. The second is that when Americans are exposed to people in need, they want to help.

Whatever else went wrong before, during, and after Katrina slammed into the American Southeast, most of the subsequent suffering in New Orleans stemmed from one oversight: no one made provisions to evacuate the poor who couldn't evacuate themselves. It happened because the people who were in charge—or should have been in charge—didn't think about the large number of poor people who lived in New Orleans and what it means to be poor in the inner city.

The city government gave an order to evacuate, and evacuation was no problem for the middle and upper classes. They just packed up their cars or headed for the airport and traveled away from the hurricane zone to stay temporarily with relatives or friends or at hotels. Tens of thousands of poor New Orleans residents didn't have cars, however. Many didn't have friends or relatives outside New Orleans with whom they could stay. They certainly didn't have enough cash to pay for hotel or motel rooms for any length of time. They couldn't afford to buy airline tickets. Many didn't even have enough money to buy bus tickets to take their families away from danger.

Unlike affluent Americans, most poor people aren't mobile. They aren't used to taking vacations around the country or around the world. They live in the same neighborhood for generations. They don't own stocks and bonds. Many don't even have a bank account. Everything they own is in their homes, which they probably don't have adequately insured. So it's much more difficult for them to pack up and leave in any circumstance. Not only can they not afford it—not only do they have no place to go—but they're reluctant to leave all of their possessions behind, unprotected in neighborhoods where crime is more common than in more affluent communities.

Most Americans didn't understand this. That's why most Americans' initial reaction toward those left stranded in New Orleans was something like, how could they have been so stupid as to stay there? As the horrors of life in flooded New Orleans became clear, the reaction changed to, how can this be happening in the United States? I was asked that question many times by Europeans as well.

I wrote earlier in this book that hunger and poverty in America differ from hunger and poverty in the third world. One difference, I wrote, is that you don't find America's poor cowering in refugee camps. Yet, for a brief time in New Orleans, that's exactly what we saw. Thousands of New Orleanians fled their flooded homes and converged on the Louisiana Superdome indoor football stadium and the enormous Ernest N. Morial Convention Center. Unlike in most third world refugee camps, however, these American refugees didn't encounter humanitarian aid workers ready to give them food, shelter, clothing, and medical care. They were completely on their own—hot, wet, dirty, hungry, perhaps ill, perhaps fearing for their health and safety or for the health and safety of their children or their elderly relatives. There was no food, no water, no electricity, no air-conditioning, no police officers, no medical personnel, no working bathrooms.

People died in these conditions, and no one was around to collect their bodies. So they were left where they died. At the convention center, one body was in a wheelchair, one on a chaise lounge, another on the ground. Other bodies were found floating in the flooded streets.

This extreme event was an aberration in America. But these people were poor before Katrina struck, and they will be poor into the future. And they have their counterparts in every big city in America and throughout rural America as well. They live on Dayton's west wide, in inner-city Detroit, in the small towns and countryside of southeastern Ohio and in the rest of Appalachia, in the southern counties of Mississippi, in central Los Angeles, on Indian reservations throughout the West, and in the shadow of the Capitol's dome in Washington, D.C., among many other places. As U.S. Senator Barack Obama of Illinois said, "The people of New Orleans weren't just abandoned during the hurricane. They were abandoned long ago—to murder and mayhem in the streets, to substandard schools, to dilapidated housing, to inadequate health care, to a pervasive sense of hopelessness." And that is true of America's other poor neighborhoods.

Nearly a quarter of New Orleans residents lived below the poverty level. In the Lower Ninth Ward, where most of the Superdome and convention center refugees had their homes, about a third were poor. In one especially hard-hit neighborhood, according to an Associated Press analysis, nearly three-quarters were poor and just one-third had a car.[1] About 120,000 residents of the New Orleans area didn't have access to a car, according to Shirley Laska of the University of New Orleans Center for Hazards Assessment, Response, and Technology.[2] Nationally, 12.7 percent of the population—thirty-seven million Americans—live in poverty, and the rate has been rising in recent years.[3] But the middle class and the rich seldom see the poor. And even when they are forced into our attention—as they were in New Orleans—we quickly forget once the drama has passed.

As much as I talked about domestic hunger while I served in Congress—as much as I called it to the attention of my constituents—even some of my best friends would say, "Tony, that can't be true. We never see many poor people."

And I'd say, "You don't see them because you don't look for them. When you drive from your home to your work, you don't see poor people on the sidewalk begging for food. You don't drive through the poorest parts of town. You don't go to the food banks and the soup kitchens. You don't talk with these people. You don't listen to these people."

When I give speeches, I tell people that nearly ten million Americans live in homes where someone frequently goes hungry, that more than twenty-five million live in homes that are at risk of hunger, that twenty to twenty-five million stave off hunger by frequenting food banks and soup kitchens. Even more disturbing, after declining during the late 1990s, these figures have been going up since 2001. My listeners scratch their heads and ask, "Where are these people? I never see these people."

To see hungry people, to see children falling asleep in class because they don't eat well, to see parents and children living on the street, you have to go look for them. And most Americans don't do that. But when you show Americans the poor and the hungry—when you connect with them and educate them and they see the problems themselves—they don't turn their backs. They want to help. They respond. We are a compassionate people, a giving people. We care. And that's the other truth about America that Hurricane Katrina revealed so dramatically.

As soon as they figured out what was happening in Katrina's wake, the American people opened their pocketbooks, their communities—even their homes—to help. Organizations all over the country raised funds for hurricane relief. Corporations contributed hundreds of millions of dollars. Other companies donated products or services of value to the relief efforts. Television networks broadcast fund-raising telethons. Employers from around the country offered jobs to the suddenly unemployed. People with potentially useful skills volunteered to travel to the affected areas to work. Communities across the country provided shelters and offered to send some of their emergency crews to help with rescue, recovery, and security efforts. Individual families invited strangers to occupy spare bedrooms in their homes.

The people also showed that they are far ahead of their political leaders when it comes to understanding what values are really important at times like this. An Associated Press survey asked where the government should find the money to pay its share of the hurricane relief costs. Only 11 percent said it should come from cutting other domestic programs, even though that is what leaders in Congress wanted to do.[4] Another survey, by the Bendixen & Associates polling firm, found that a plurality of Americans believe our top priority as a nation should be fighting poverty.[5]

If we could sustain this level of awareness and concern beyond the immediate aftermath of the New Orleans tragedy, the goals of ending hunger and poverty really could be achieved. And it really wouldn't be that hard.

I've learned through my work over the last two decades that none of us has to take the burden of the entire world on our shoulders. None of us has to solve every problem. As Mother Teresa taught me, we just have to do the thing that's in front of us. Millions of people did that in the aftermath of Hurricane Katrina. Some did a great deal—leaving their homes, traveling to the disaster scene, working day and night for an extended time to help in the relief efforts. Others did a little bit—contributing a small amount of money to a humanitarian organization, for example. They all did what they could. Together, that amounted to a great deal.

That's all we have to do to wage an effective fight against hunger and poverty and oppression around the world—do what's in front of us. For some, that will mean joining a humanitarian organization and setting off for a strange land to work with the poor and the hungry in a place like the Congo or Rwanda. For others, it will mean leaving home to work with disadvantaged Americans in an inner city or up in an Appalachian hollow or on an Indian reservation. For yet others, it will mean volunteering close to home at a food bank, tutoring poor children in a local school, or helping at a homeless shelter a couple of nights a month. Some will join campaigns to demand that the government do more for the poor, the hungry, and the oppressed. Some will work to elect candidates who are committed to helping "the least of these." Some will run for office themselves. Others will simply visit an elderly shut-in up the street or write a check to a respected charity.

Together, they will change the world.

What will you do?

HOW TO HELP

I t's easy to join the many people who give some of their time and treasure to help the less fortunate. All you have to do is look around you, find someone with a need, and address it. It can be as simple as visiting with a lonely elderly neighbor, saying kind words to a child who is unpopular at school, or giving blood to the Red Cross. You can donate money to a good cause. You can volunteer to help out at a food bank or work in your church's clothing drive. If you see a need that isn't being addressed, you can get together with friends and neighbors and create an organization to address it. Many of the most effective humanitarian organizations in the world started out exactly that way.

It you'd rather get involved with an established national or international organization, here's a list of some of the best. All accept financial contributions. Some accept volunteers. Most employ humanitarian workers. You can learn more about them by visiting their Internet sites.

Bread for the World: Christian organization that campaigns for government programs to address hunger. Membership includes fifty-four thousand individuals and twenty-five hundred Catholic, Protestant, and Orthodox churches. Members lobby their U.S. representatives and senators. Bread for the World Institute carries out research and educational projects, including an annual report on hunger. 50 F St. NW, Suite 500, Washington, DC 20001. Phone 202-639-9400 or 800-822-7323. Fax 202-639-9401. www.bread.org.

CARE: Founded in 1945 to ship CARE Packages of relief supplies to survivors of World War II. Now runs a wide range of emergency relief and long-term development programs in more than seventy countries. Offers short-term volunteer experiences through CARE Corps Abroad. 151 Ellis St., Atlanta, GA 30303. Phone 404-681-2552 or 800-521-2273. Fax 404-589-2651. www.care.org.

Carter Center: Established in 1982 and still led by former president and first lady Jimmy and Rosalynn Carter. Operates projects around the world to advance peace and human rights, promote democracy, and fight poverty, disease, and hunger. Some volunteer opportunities at headquarters. 453 Freedom Pkwy., Atlanta, GA 30307. Phone 404-420-5100. www.cartercenter.org.

Catholic Relief Services: Official international relief and development agency of the Catholic Church in the United States. Provides emergency relief and development assistance in more than ninety countries. Offers numerous opportunities for Catholics to become involved in the agency's work. 209 W. Fayette St., Baltimore, MD 21201. Phone 410-625-2220 or 800-736-3467. www.catholicrelief.org.

Church World Service: Relief and development ministry of thirty-six Protestant, Orthodox, and Anglican denominations in the United States. Works with indigenous organizations in more than eighty countries to meet emergency needs and promote self-reliance. Offers volunteer opportunities with local affiliates in the United States. Organizes campaigns to influence U.S. government policies. 28606 Phillips St., P.O. Box 968, Elkhart, IN 46515. Phone 800-297-1516. www.churchworldservice.org.

Concern: Organized in Ireland in response to the Biafra famine in 1968. Carries out emergency relief and long-term development projects in more than twenty-five countries, most in Africa and Asia. Headquartered in Dublin, with offices in Belfast, London, and Glasgow and an affiliated organization in the United States. Offers volunteer opportunities in Ireland and the United States. 52-55 Lower Camden St., Dublin 2, Republic of Ireland. Phone 353-1-417-7700. Fax 353-1-475-7362. www.concern.net. U.S. affiliate: 104 E. 40th

St., Suite 903, New York, NY 10016. Phone 212-557-8000. Fax 212-557-8004. www.concernusa.org.

Congressional Hunger Center: Nonpartisan antihunger organization related to but independent of Congress. Develops tomorrow's humanitarian leaders through training and internship programs that place dedicated young people in internships with humanitarian organizations in the United States and around the world. 229 Pennsylvania Ave. SE, Washington, DC 20003. Phone 202-547-7022. Fax 202-547-7575. www.hungercenter.org.

Doctors without Borders: Deploys volunteer medical and support personnel, along with locally hired staff, to deliver emergency health care in more than seventy countries. Recruits volunteer doctors, nurses, midwives, laboratory technicians, logisticians, water and sanitation specialists, and financial managers. Also uses volunteers in U.S. offices. 333 7th Ave., 2nd Floor, New York, NY 10001-5004. Phone 212-679-6800. Fax 212-679-7016. www.doctorswithoutborders.org.

Feed the Children: Christian organization that distributes food, medicine, clothing, and other necessities to needy families in all fifty states and fifty seven foreign countries. Accepts donations of food and other supplies from corporations and cash contributions from individuals. Also operates long-term programs to help people become self-sufficient. Encourages churches and other nonprofit organizations to become partner agencies to deliver food in their communities. Offers a wide range of volunteer opportunities, from conducting a small fund-raising event at home to working in the field in projects in the United States and overseas. P.O. Box 36, Oklahoma City, OK 73101-0036. Phone 800-627-4556. Fax 405-945-4177. www.feedthechildren.org.

Food for the Hungry: Christian organization that ministers to the physical and spiritual needs of the poor by providing emergency relief as well as operating child development, agriculture, clean water, health, nutrition, education, and microenterprise programs in more than forty-five countries. Offers a variety of volunteer opportunities at home and abroad. 1224 E. Washington St., Phoenix, AZ 85034-1102. Phone 480-998-310 or 800-248-6437. www.fh.org.

Global Witness: Investigative organization that exposes links between natural resource exploitation and human rights abuses—the trade in blood diamonds, for example. Gathers evidence and presents it to governments, private organizations, donors, development organizations, the media, and the general public to promote an end to the exploitation. Provides opportunities for individuals to join its lobbying campaigns. P.O. Box 6042, London, N19 5WP, United Kingdom. Phone 44-020-7272-6731. Fax 44-020-7272-9425. U.S. office: 1120 19th St. NW, 8th Floor, Washington, DC 20036. Phone 202-721-5670. Fax 202-530-0128. www.globalwitness.org.

Heifer Project International: Provides livestock, financial assistance, training, and other aid to poor families and communities in the United States and overseas to help them become self-sufficient. Heifer's unique fund-raising scheme enables individuals and organizations to purchase specific livestock (a heifer, for instance) for the poor. Also offers opportunities for individuals to volunteer and businesses to enter Heifer partnerships. P.O. Box 8058, Little Rock, AR 72203. Phone 800-422-0474. www.heifer.org.

Helen Keller International: Assists the blind and visually impaired and fights the causes of blindness in twenty-five countries. Activities include screening, education, treatment, distribution of nutritious food, agriculture development, and prenatal care. Also conducts research, advises governments, and helps establish sustainable programs. 352 Park Ave. S., 12th Floor, New York, NY 10010. Phone 212-532-0544 or 877-535-5374. Fax 212-532-6014. www.hki.org.

International Justice Mission: Works to free victims of violence, sexual exploitation, slavery, and oppression and to bring perpetrators to justice. Trains police in combating sex trafficking. Helps communities prepare to deter abuse. Assists victims in recovery. Offers internships to law students and encourages students to organize college campus chapters. P.O. Box 58147, Washington, DC 20037-8147. Phone 703-465-5495. Fax 703-465-5499. www.ijm.org.

International Polio Victims Response Committee: U.S.-registered, tax-exempt charity that raises funds for Jay Nash's Congolese Association for Orthopedic

Assistance to Young People. ACAOJH (the Congolese Association's French acronym) supplies braces to polio victims in the Congo. 10250 Harrison Rd., Loveland, OH 45140. www.congo-pages.org/ipvrc/home.htm.

Mercy Corps: Operates emergency relief and long-term development programs in thirty-five countries. Works to end and prevent conflicts by bringing together representatives of diverse groups and promoting democracy, citizen participation, and the rule of law. Offers internships for students preparing for careers in international development. Provides volunteer opportunities at headquarters in Portland. Organizes supporters to advocate government action to benefit the poor. Helps supporters conduct fund-raising events. Department W, P.O. Box 2669, Portland, OR 97208-2669. Phone 888-256-1900. www.mercycorps.org.

Opportunity International: Promotes microenterprise development by providing small loans, savings programs, insurance benefits, training and personal counseling to poor people in Africa, Asia, Eastern Europe, and Latin America. Accepts contributions and offers some volunteer opportunities. 2122 York Rd., Oak Brook, IL 60523. Phone 800-793-9455. Fax 630-645-1458. www.opportunity.org.

Operation Smile: Sends volunteer medical personnel around the world to provide reconstructive surgery and related health care to poor children and young adults. Also advocates for sustainable health-care systems. Offers volunteer opportunities for professionals with medical skills such as plastic surgery, anesthesiology, pediatrics, dentistry, and speech pathology, as well as for biomedical technicians, child life specialists, and medical students. Forms partnerships with service clubs and corporations that donate supplies and services. Helps supporters organize fund-raising events. 6435 Tidewater Dr., Norfolk, VA 23509. Phone 757-321-7645. Fax 757-321-7660. www.operationsmile.org.

Prison Fellowship International: Founded in 1976 by Charles W. Colson, former chief counsel to President Nixon, who was imprisoned for his role in the Watergate scandal. Provides support services to 100,000 volunteers in 112 prison fellowship organizations that conduct Christian missions to prisoners, ex-prisoners, crime victims, and their families around the world. Organization's goal is to restore offenders to meaningful roles in society. Offers extensive volunteer opportunities with its affiliated fellowships. P.O. Box 17434, Washington, DC 20041. Phone 703-481-0000. www.pfi.org.

Project Mercy: Comprehensive development project to help the residents of Yetebon, Ethiopia, become self-sufficient. Has built a school, hospital, day-care center, irrigation system, and houses there. Provides adult education in agriculture, carpentry, metalworking, basket making, embroidery, spinning, and other useful skills. Uses skilled volunteers in such fields as teaching, information technology, carpentry, cooking, sanitation, and health care. Organizes volunteer expeditions with church groups. 7011 Ardmore Ave., Fort Wayne, IN 46809. Phone 260-747-2559. Fax 260-478-1361. www.projectmercy.org.

RESULTS: Grassroots advocacy organization that promotes government policies to fight hunger and poverty. Works in United States and six other countries. Lobbies public officials, conducts research, and communicates with the media and the general public. Has one hundred local chapters in the United States plus individual activists throughout the country. Volunteer opportunities range from becoming active in a local chapter to contacting public officials in response to e-mail alerts. 440 First St. NW, Suite 450, Washington, DC 20001. Phone 202-783-7100. www.results.org.

Salvation Army: Evangelical Christian movement, founded in London in 1865, that serves the poor throughout the world. Provides a wide range of emergency relief and other services in more than one hundred countries. Offers extensive volunteer opportunities. 101 Queen Victoria St., London EC4P 4EP, England. Phone 44-20-7332-0101. Fax 44-20-7236-4681. U.S. headquarters: P.O. Box 269, Alexandria, VA 22313. Phone 703-684 5500. Fax 703-684-3478. www.salvationarmy.org.

Save the Children: U.S. member of International Save the Children Alliance of 27 national organizations working in more than 110 countries. U.S. unit works in the poorest communities in 12 states and in more than 45 countries. Services, which promote child well-being and family self-sufficiency, include literacy, physical activity, nutrition, microenterprise, agricultural development, reproductive health, newborn and child health, parent education, early childhood development, and emergency relief. Offers volunteer opportunities in U.S. projects. Organizes supporters to advocate for government programs that help children. Fosters long-term partnerships with corporations. 54 Wilton Rd., Westport, CT 06880. Phone 203-221-4030 or 800-728-3843. www.savethechildren.org. International Internet site: www.savethechildren.net.

World Vision: Christian relief and development organization focused especially on the needs of children. Operates emergency relief, education, healthcare, and economic and agricultural development programs around the world through national affiliates. U.S. affiliate offers volunteer opportunities and partnerships with churches and corporations. U.S. headquarters: P.O. Box 9716, Federal Way, WA 98063-9716. Phone 253-815-1000 or 888-511-6548. www.worldvision.org. International Internet site: www.wvi.org.

NOTES

CHAPTER 3

1. Pope John Paul II, "Letter on the Occasion of the 50th Anniversary of the Foundation of the Missionaries of Charity," October 2, 2000, www.vatican.va/holy_father/john_paul_ii/letters/2000/documents/hf_jp-ii_let_20001017_missionaries-charity_en.html.

2. Cooper, Kenneth J., "Mother Teresa Dies at 87," *Washington Post,* September 6, 1997, A1.

3. Muhammad Yunus, "The Commonwealth Lecture," 2003, www.grameen-info.org/bank/Commonlth01.html.

4. Ibid.

5. "Grameen Bank at a Glance," Grameen Bank, September 2005, www.grameen-info.org/bank/GBGlance.htm.

6. Muhammad Yunus, "Muhammad Yunus Reflects on Working Toward Peace," Architects of Peace Project, Santa Clara University, Santa Clara, CA, www.scu.edu/ethics/architects-of-peace/Yunus/essay.html.

7. "Grameen Bank at a Glance."

8. Ibid.

9. David Bornstein, *How to Change the World* (Oxford: Oxford University Press, 2004),14.

10. Muhammad Yunus, "On the Occasion of Receiving the Planetary Consciousness Business Innovation Prize 1997 of the Club of Budapest," www.grameen-info.org/agrameen/speech.php3?speech=5.

11. Muhammad Yunus, *Banker to the Poor,* (New York: Public Affairs, 1999).

12. Ibid.

13. Lyla Bashan, "Eradicating Poverty One Loan at a Time," Global Envision, www.globalenvision.org/library/4/261/.

14. Frances Schwartzkopff, "Lending on Faith," *Atlanta Constitution,* March 14, 1993, H1. "Mini-Loans in Mini-Towns Produce Mini-Businesses," *Christian Science Monitor,* March 26, 1993.

15. Yunus, "Commonwealth Lecture."

CHAPTER 5

1. Gheorghe Calciu, "Delivered from the Lion's Den," remarks to conference sponsored by the Christian Relief Effort for the Emancipation of Dissidents, Washington, DC, November 9, 1985, www.roca.org/OA/55/55b.htm.

2. Richard Higgins, "A Sermon of Faith, Bridging Oppression," *Boston Globe*, March 12, 1990, 15.

3. "Bishop Lazlo Tokes on Spiritual Loss and Spiritual Gain," East-West Church & Ministry Report, Winter 1994, www.samford.edu/groups/global/ewcmreport/articles/ew02112.htm.

4. Calciu, "Delivered from the Lion's Den."

CHAPTER 6

1. "Tony Hall's Fast," *Roll Call*, April 5, 1993, 4.

2. Richard Blow, "Life in the Fast Lane," *Washington Post*, April 16, 1993, B1.

3. Quoted in Tom Price, "House Welcomes Hall with Pledge of Action," *Dayton Daily News*, April 29, 1993, p.1.

4. Quoted in ibid.

5. Quoted in ibid.

CHAPTER 8

1. "Domestic Hunger and Poverty Facts," Bread for the World Institute, 2005, www.bread.org/hungerbasics/domestic.html.

2. "Household Food Security in the United States, 2003," Research Briefs, United States Department of Agriculture, www.ers.usda.gov/publications/fanrr42/fanrr42_researchbrief.pdf.

CHAPTER 10

1. "Faith Communities Today," Hartford Institute for Religion Research, Hartford Seminary, Hartford, CT, March 2001, www.fact.hartsem.edu/research/fact2000/Final%20FACTrpt.pdf.

2. "The Mosque in America: A National Portrait," Council on American-Islamic Relations, Washington, DC, April 25, 2001, www.cair-net.org/mosquereport/Mosque_Community_Services.htm.

3. "USDA Conducts National Study of Food Pantries," United States Department of Agriculture, July 2003, www.pahunger.org/html/hunger/ArchPDF/USDA_Conducts_National_Study_of_Food_Pantries.pdf.

4. "About MAZON," MAZON: A Jewish Response to Hunger, www.Mazon.org/Who_we_Are/About_MAZON/index.asp.

5. Muhammad Yunus, *Banker to the Poor* (New York: Public Affairs, 1999), www.grameen-info.org/book/index.htm.

6. "Grameen Bank at a Glance," Grameen Bank, September 2005, www.grameen-info.org/bank/GBGlance.htm.

7. Yunus, *Banker to the Poor*.

8. Laxminarayan, Ramdas, "Dismantling Prejudice: The Journey to a People Based Peace Strategy," Magsaysay Awardees' Lecture Series, Manila, August 27, 2004, www.rmaf.org.ph/Awardees/Lecture/LectureRamdasLax.htm.

9. Tihomir Kukolja, posted on Web page that is no longer active.

10. "Faith Communities Today."

11. "For the Health of the Nation: An Evangelical Call to Civic Responsibiltiy," National Association of Evangelicals, October 2004, www.nae.net/images/ civic_responsibility2.pdf.

12. Ibid.

13. Ibid.

14. Ibid.

15. Quoted in Alan Cooperman "Religious Right, Left Meet in Middle," Washington Post, June 15, 2005, A1.

16. "Interview: Richard Cizik, National Association of Evangelicals," *Christian Post,* July 11, 2005, www.christianpost.com/article/church/2160/section/ interview.richard.cizik.national.association.of.evangelicals/1.htm

17. Njongonkulu W. H., Ndungane, keynote address at "Hunger No More: An Interfaith Convocation," Washington National Cathedral, Washington, DC, June 6, 2005, www.cathedral.org/cathedral/programs/hungernomore/ndunganekeynote.html.

TONY HALL

Nominated three times for the Nobel Peace Prize, Tony Hall is widely recognized as one of the world's leading advocates for the hungry, the poor, and the oppressed. A former Democratic congressman who was appointed ambassador to the United Nations food and agricultural agencies by Republican president George W. Bush, Hall works closely with people of all political persuasions and religious faiths. He has traveled to more than one hundred countries, from Afghanistan to Zimbabwe, to investigate the needs of the poor and to urge the affluent to help.

Hall was born and reared in the Dayton, Ohio, area. He earned a bachelor of arts degree at Denison University, where he was a Little All-American football player, then served in the Peace Corps in Thailand. He was elected to the Ohio House of Representatives and the Ohio Senate before becoming Dayton's U.S. representative. In Congress from 1979 through 2002, he helped found and became chairman of the House Select Committee on Hunger and was an influential member of the powerful Rules Committee. In what began as an act of personal witness, Hall fasted for twenty-two days in 1993 to call attention to hunger and was astonished at the enormous positive public response. He has traveled to North Korea six times—more than any other elected official from the West—to investigate hunger in the reclusive Communist dictatorship. He was instrumental in bringing the United States and the Soviet Union together to combat famine in Ethiopia at the end of the Cold War in 1990. In 2004 he helped to broker a deal in which Libya opened its borders so that U.S. food could be shipped to hungry refugees in Sudan and Chad.

Hall and his wife, Janet, have reared two children, a daughter, Jyl, who is beginning a career ministering to the disadvantaged, and a son, Matt, who died of leukemia at age fifteen in 1996.

TOM PRICE

T om Price is a veteran journalist who has written about Tony Hall since 1975, when Hall was an Ohio state senator from Dayton and Price was a reporter for the Dayton *Journal Herald*. In 1982 Price became a correspondent in the Cox Newspapers Washington Bureau, where he continued to cover Hall's congressional career. He has been a Washington-based freelance journalist since 1996. With his wife, Susan, he is coauthor of the award-winning *The Working Parents Help Book*. He also has written two Washington guidebooks. The Prices' daughter, Julie, is a student at the College of William and Mary.

**THE CAMPAIGN TO MAKE
POVERTY HISTORY
WWW.ONE.ORG**

There is a plague of biblical proportions taking place in Africa right now, but we can beat this crisis, if we each do our part. The first step is signing the ONE Declaration to join the ONE Campaign.

The ONE Campaign is a new effort to rally Americans, ONE by ONE, to fight the emergency of global AIDS and extreme poverty. We are engaging Americans everywhere we gather—in churches and synagogues, on the internet and college campuses, at community meetings and concerts.

"All we have to do to wage an effective fight against hunger, poverty, and oppression around the world—do what's in front of us. . . . Some will join campaigns to demand that the government do more for the poor, the hungry, and the oppressed. . . .Together, they will change the world. What will you do?"

—Tony Hall, *Changing the Face of Hunger*

Together, we can all make a difference in the lives of the poorest of God's children.

We invite you to join the ONE Campaign.
To learn more about ONE, please visit WWW.ONE.ORG.

**ONE Voice can make a difference.
Join the ONE Campaign now!**

This campaign is brought to you by

D ATA aims to raise awareness about, and spark response to the crises swamping Africa: unpayable debts, uncontrolled spread of AIDS, and unfair trade rules which keep Africans poor. DATA calls on the governments of the world's wealthiest nations to put more resources toward Africa and to adopt policy that helps rather than hinders Africa in achieving long-term prosperity. DATA also calls on Africa's leaders to strengthen Democracy, Accountability and Transparency toward their own citizens—to make sure that support for African people goes where it's intended and makes a real difference. DATA was co-founded by Bono of U2 and Bobby Shriver and is a founding member of The ONE Campaign. 1400 Eye St, NW, Suite 1125, Washington DC 20005. p202-639-8010, f202-639-8011, www.data.org.